TEACHER'S PET PUBLICATIONS

LITPLAN TEACHER PACK
for
The Tempest
based on the play by
William Shakespeare

Written by
Mary B. Collins

© 1994 Teacher's Pet Publications
All Rights Reserved

This **LitPlan** for William Shakespeare's
The Tempest
has been brought to you by Teacher's Pet Publications, Inc.

Copyright Teacher's Pet Publications 1994
11504 Hammock Point
Berlin MD 21811

Only the student materials in this unit plan (such as worksheets,
study questions, and tests) may be reproduced multiple times
for use in the purchaser's classroom.

For any additional copyright questions,
contact Teacher's Pet Publications.

www.tpet.com

TABLE OF CONTENTS - *Tempest*

Introduction	11
Unit Objectives	13
Reading Assignment Sheet	14
Unit Outline	15
Study Questions (Short Answer)	19
Quiz/Study Questions (Multiple Choice)	23
Pre-reading Vocabulary Worksheets	31
Lesson One (Introductory Lesson)	45
Nonfiction Assignment Sheet	48
Oral Reading Evaluation Form	51
Writing Assignment 1	53
Writing Assignment 2	61
Writing Assignment 3	65
Writing Evaluation Form	64
Vocabulary Review Activities	60
Extra Writing Assignments/Discussion ?s	56
Unit Review Activities	66
Unit Tests	69
Unit Resource Materials	103
Vocabulary Resource Materials	119

ABOUT THE AUTHOR
WILLIAM SHAKESPEARE

SHAKESPEARE, William (1564-1616). For more than 350 years, William Shakespeare has been the world's most popular playwright. On the stage, in the movies, and on television his plays are watched by vast audiences. People read his plays again and again for pleasure. Students reading his plays for the first time are delighted by what they find.

Shakespeare's continued popularity is due to many things. His plays are filled with action, his characters are believable, and his language is thrilling to hear or read. Underlying all this is Shakespeare's deep humanity. He was a profound student of people and he understood them. He had a great tolerance, sympathy, and love for all people, good or evil.

While watching a Shakespearean tragedy, the audience is moved and shaken. After the show the spectators are calm, washed clean of pity and terror. They are saddened but at peace, repeating the old saying, "There, but for the grace of God, go I."

A Shakespearean comedy is full of fun. The characters are lively; the dialogue is witty. In the end young lovers are wed; old babblers are silenced; wise men are content. The comedies are joyous and romantic.

Boyhood in Stratford

William Shakespeare was born in Stratford-upon-Avon, England, in 1564. This was the sixth year of the reign of Queen Elizabeth I. He was christened on April 26 of that year. The day of his birth is unknown. It has long been celebrated on April 23, the feast of St. George.

He was the third child and oldest son of John and Mary Arden Shakespeare. Two sisters, Joan and Margaret, died before he was born. The other children were Gilbert, a second Joan, Anne, Richard, and Edmund. Only the second Joan outlived William.

Shakespeare's father was a tanner and glovemaker. He was an alderman of Stratford for years. He also served a term as high bailiff, or mayor. Toward the end of his life John Shakespeare lost most of his money. When he died in 1601, he left William only a little real estate. Not much is known about Mary Shakespeare, except that she came from a wealthier family than her husband.

Stratford-upon-Avon is in Warwickshire, called the heart of England. In Shakespeare's day it was well farmed and heavily wooded. The town itself was prosperous and progressive.

The town was proud of its grammar school. Young Shakespeare went to it, although when or for how long is not known. He may have been a pupil there between his 7th and 13th years. His studies must have been mainly in Latin. The schooling was good. All four schoolmasters at the school during Shakespeare's boyhood were graduates of Oxford University.

Nothing definite is known about his boyhood. From the content of his plays, he must have learned early about the woods and fields, about birds, insects, and small animals, about trades and outdoor sports, and about the country people he later portrayed with such good humor. Then and later he picked up an amazing stock of facts about hunting, hawking, fishing, dances, music, and other arts and sports. Among other subjects, he also learned about alchemy, astrology, folklore, medicine, and law. As good writers do, he collected information both from books and
from daily observation of the world around him.

Marriage and Life in London
In 1582, when he was 18, he married Anne Hathaway. She was from Shottery, a village a mile from Stratford. Anne was seven or eight years older than Shakespeare. From this difference in their ages, a story arose that they were unhappy together. Their first daughter, Susanna, was
born in 1583. In 1585 a twin boy and girl, Hamnet and Judith, were born.

What Shakespeare did between 1583 and 1592 is not known. Various stories are told. He may have taught school, worked in a lawyer's office, served on a rich man's estate, or traveled with a company of actors. One famous story says that about 1584 he and some friends were caught poaching on the estate of Sir Thomas Lucy of Carlecote, near Warwick, and were forced to leave town. A less likely story is that he was in London in 1588. There he was supposed to have held horses for theater patrons and later to have worked in the theaters as a callboy.

By 1592, however, Shakespeare was definitely in London and was already recognized as an actor and playwright. He was then 28 years old. In that year he was referred to in another man's book for the first time. Robert Greene, a playwright, accused him of borrowing from the plays of
others.

Between 1592 and 1594, plague kept the London theaters closed most of the time. During these years Shakespeare wrote his earliest sonnets and two long narrative poems, 'Venus and Adonis' and 'The Rape of Lucrece'. Both were printed by Richard Field, a boyhood friend from Stratford. They were well received and helped establish him as a poet.

Shakespeare Prospers
Until 1598 Shakespeare's theater work was confined to a district northeast of London. This was outside the walls, in the parish of Shoreditch. Located there were two playhouses, the Theatre and the Curtain. Both were managed by James Burbage, whose son Richard Burbage was Shakespeare's friend and the greatest tragic actor of his day.

Up to 1596 Shakespeare lived near these theaters in Bishopsgate, where the North Road entered the city. Sometime between 1596 and 1599, he moved across the Thames River to a district called Bankside. There, two theaters, the Rose and the Swan, had been built by Philip Henslowe. He was James Burbage's chief competitor in London as a theater manager.

The Burbages also moved to this district in 1598 and built the famous Globe Theatre. Its sign showed Atlas supporting the world-hence the theater's name. Shakespeare was associated with the Globe Theatre for the rest of his active life. He owned shares in it, which brought him much money.

Meanwhile, in 1597, Shakespeare had bought New Place, the largest house in Stratford. During the next three years he bought other property in Stratford and in London. The year before, his father, probably at Shakespeare's suggestion, applied for and was granted a coat of arms. It bore the motto Non sanz droict-Not without right. From this time on, Shakespeare could write "Gentleman" after his name. This meant much to him, for in his day actors were classed legally with criminals and vagrants.

Shakespeare's name first appeared on the title pages of his printed plays in 1598. In the same year Francis Meres, in 'Palladis Tamia: Wit's Treasury', praised him as a poet and dramatist. Meres's comments on 12 of Shakespeare's plays showed that Shakespeare's genius was recognized in his own time.

Honored As Actor and Playwright

Queen Elizabeth I died in 1603. King James I followed her to the throne. Shakespeare's theatrical company was taken under the king's patronage and called the King's Company. Shakespeare and the other actors were made officers of the royal household. The theatrical company was the most successful of its time. Before it was the King's Company, it had been known as the Earl of Derby's and the Lord Chamberlain's. In 1608 the company acquired the Blackfriars Theatre. This was a smaller and more aristocratic theater than the Globe. Thereafter the company alternated between the two playhouses.

Plays by Shakespeare were performed at both theaters, at the royal court, and in the castles of the nobles. After 1603 Shakespeare probably acted little, although he was still a good actor. His favorite roles seem to have been old Adam in 'As You Like It' and the Ghost in 'Hamlet'.

In 1607, when he was 43, he may have suffered a serious physical breakdown. In the same year his older daughter Susanna married John Hall, a doctor. The next year Shakespeare's first grandchild, Elizabeth, was born. Also in 1607 his brother Edmund, who had been an actor in London, died at the age of 27.

The Mermaid Tavern Group

About this time Shakespeare became one of the group of now-famous writers who gathered at the Mermaid Tavern in Cheapside. The club was formed by Sir Walter Raleigh. Ben Jonson was its leading spirit (see Jonson). Shakespeare was a popular member. He was admired for his talent and loved for his kindliness. Thomas Fuller, writing about 50 years later, gave an amusing account of the conversational duels between Shakespeare and Jonson:

"Many were the wit-combats betwixt him and Ben Jonson; which two I behold like a Spanish great galleon and an English man-of-war; Master Jonson (like the former) was built far higher in learning; solid, but slow, in his performances. Shakespeare, with the English man-of-war, lesser in bulk, but lighter in sailing, could turn with all tides, tack about, and take advantage of all winds, by the quickness of his wit and invention."

Jonson sometimes criticized Shakespeare harshly. Nevertheless he later wrote a eulogy of Shakespeare that is remarkable for its feeling and acuteness. In it he said:

> Leave thee alone, for the comparison
> Of all that insolent Greece or haughty Rome
> Sent forth, or since did from their ashes come.
> Triumph, my Britain, thou hast one to show
> To whom all scenes of Europe homage owe.
> He was not of an age, but for all time!
> . . . .
> Sweet Swan of Avon! what a sight it were
> To see thee in our waters yet appear,
> And make those flights upon the banks of Thames,
> That so did take Eliza, and our James!

Death and Burial at Stratford

Shakespeare retired from his theater work in 1610 and returned to Stratford. His friends from London visited him. In 1613 the Globe Theatre burned. He lost much money in it, but he was still wealthy. He shared in the building of the new Globe. A few months before the fire he bought as an investment a house in the fashionable Blackfriars district of London.

On April 23, 1616, Shakespeare died at the age of 52. This date is according to the Old Style, or Julian, calendar of his time. The New Style, or Gregorian, calendar date is May 3, 1616. He was buried in the chancel of the Church of the Holy Trinity in Stratford.

A stone slab-a reproduction of the original one, which it replaced in 1830-marks his grave. It bears an inscription, perhaps written by himself.

On the north wall of the chancel is his monument. It consists of a portrait bust enclosed in a stone frame. Below it is an inscription in Latin and English. This bust and the engraving by Martin Droeshout, prefixed to the First Folio edition of his plays (1623), are the only pictures of Shakespeare which can be accepted as showing his true likeness.

John Aubrey, an English antiquarian, wrote about Shakespeare 65 years after the poet's death. He evidently used information furnished by the son of one of Shakespeare's fellow actors. Aubrey described him as "a handsome, well-shaped man, very good company, and of a ready and pleasant smooth wit."

Shakespeare's will, still in existence, bequeathed most of his property to Susanna and her daughter. He left small mementoes to friends. He mentioned his wife only once, leaving her his "second best bed" with its furnishings.

Much has been written about this odd bequest. There is little reason to think it was a slight. Indeed, it may have been a special mark of affection. The "second best bed" was probably the one they used. The best bed was reserved for guests. At any rate, his wife was entitled by law to one third of her husband's goods and real estate and to the use of their home for life. She died in 1623.

The will contains three signatures of Shakespeare. These, with three others, are the only known specimens of his handwriting in existence. Several experts also regard some lines in the manuscript of 'Sir Thomas More' as Shakespeare's own handwriting. He spelled his name in
various ways. His father's papers show about 16 spellings. Shakspere, Shaxpere, and Shakespeare are the most common.

Did Shakespeare Really Write the Plays?
The outward events of Shakespeare's life are ordinary. He was hard-working, sober, and middle-class in his ways. He steadily gathered wealth and took good care of his family. Many people have found it impossible to believe that such a man could have written the plays. They feel that he could not have known such heights and depths of passion. They believe that the people around Shakespeare expressed little realization of his greatness. Some say that a man of his little schooling could not have learned about the professions, the aristocratic sports of hawking and hunting, the speech and manners of the upper classes.

Since the 1800's there has been a steady effort to prove that Shakespeare did not write the plays or that others did. For a long time the leading candidate was Sir Francis Bacon. Books on the Shakespeare-Bacon argument would fill a library (see Bacon, Francis). After Bacon became less popular, the Earl of Oxford and then other men were suggested as the authors. Nearly every famous Elizabethan was named. The most recent has been Christopher Marlowe. Some people even claim that "Shakespeare" is an assumed name for a whole group of poets and playwrights.

However, some men around Shakespeare-for example, Meres in 1598 and Jonson in 1623-did recognize his worth as a man and as a writer. To argue that an obscure Stratford boy could not have become the Shakespeare of literature is to ignore the mystery of genius. His knowledge is of the kind that could not be learned in school. It is the kind that only a genius could learn, by applying a keen intelligence to everyday life. Some great writers have had even less schooling than Shakespeare.

Few scholars take seriously these attempts to deprive Shakespeare of credit. Shakespeare's style is individual and cannot be imitated. Any good student recognizes it. It can be found nowhere else. Bacon is a poor candidate for the honor. Great as he was, he was certainly not a poet.

How the Plays Came Down to Us
Since the 1700's scholars have worked over the text of Shakespeare's plays. They have had to do so because the plays were badly printed, and no original manuscripts of them survive.

In Shakespeare's day plays were not usually printed under the author's supervision. When a playwright sold a play to his company, he lost all rights to it. He could not sell it again to a publisher without the company's consent. When the play was no longer in demand on the stage, the company itself might sell the manuscript. Plays were eagerly read by the Elizabethan public. This was even more true during the plague years, when the theaters were closed. It was also true during times of business depression. Sometimes plays were taken down in shorthand and sold. At other times, a dismissed actor would write down the play from memory and sell it.

About half of Shakespeare's plays were printed during his lifetime in small, cheap pamphlets called quartos. Most of these were made from fairly accurate manuscripts. A few were in garbled form.

In 1623, seven years after Shakespeare's death, his collected plays were published in a large, expensive volume called the First Folio. It contains all his plays except two of which he wrote only part-'Pericles' and 'Two Noble Kinsmen'. It also has the first engraved portrait of Shakespeare.

This edition was authorized by Shakespeare's acting group, the King's Company. Some of the plays in it were printed from the accurate quartos and some from manuscripts in the theater. It is certain that many of these manuscripts were in Shakespeare's own handwriting. Others were copies. Still others, like the 'Tempest' manuscript, had been revised by another dramatist.

Shakespearean scholars have been determining what Shakespeare actually wrote. They have done so by studying the language, stagecraft, handwriting, and printing of the period and by carefully examining and comparing the different editions. They have modernized spelling and punctuation, supplied stage directions, explained difficult passages, and made the plays easier for the modern reader to understand.

Another hard task has been to find out when the plays were written. About half of them have no definite date of composition. The plays themselves have been searched for clues. Other books have been examined. Scholars have tried to match events in Shakespeare's life with the subject matter of his plays.

These scholars have used detective methods. They have worked with clues, deduction, shrewd reasoning, and external and internal evidence. External evidence consists of actual references in other books. Internal evidence is made up of verse tests and a study of the poet's imagery and figures of speech, which changed from year to year.

The verse tests follow the idea that a poet becomes more skillful with practice. Scholars long ago noticed that in his early plays Shakespeare used little prose, much rhyme, and certain types of rhythmical and metrical regularity. As he grew older he used more prose, less rhyme, and greater freedom and variety in rhythm and meter. From these facts, scholars have figured out the dates of those plays that had none.

Shakespeare As a Dramatist
The facts about Shakespeare are interesting in themselves, but they have little to do with his place in literature. Shakespeare wrote his plays to give pleasure. It is possible to spoil that pleasure by giving too much attention to his life, his times, and the problem of figuring out what he actually wrote. He can be enjoyed in book form, in the theater, or on television without our knowing any of these things.

Some difficulties stand in the way of this enjoyment. Shakespeare wrote more than 350 years ago. The language he used is naturally somewhat different from the language of today. Besides, he wrote in verse. Verse permits a free use of words that may not be understood by some readers. His plays are often fanciful. This may not appeal to matter-of-fact people who are used to modern realism. For all these reasons, readers may find him difficult. The worst handicap to enjoyment is the notion that Shakespeare is a "classic," a writer to be approached with awe.

The way to escape this last difficulty is to remember that Shakespeare wrote his plays for everyday people and that many in the audience were uneducated. They looked upon him as a funny, exciting, and lovable entertainer, not as a great poet. People today should read him as the people in his day listened to him. The excitement and enjoyment of the plays will banish most of the difficulties.

--- Courtesy of Compton's Learning Company

INTRODUCTION - *The Tempest*

This unit has been designed to develop students' reading, writing, thinking, and language skills through exercises and activities related to *The Tempest* by William Shakespeare. It includes twenty-four lessons, supported by extra resource materials.

The **introductory lesson** introduces students to the theme of illusion versus reality. Following the introductory activity, students are given a transition to explain how the activity relates to the play they are about to read. Following the transition, students are given the materials they will be using during the unit. At the end of the lesson, students begin the pre-reading work for the first reading assignment.

The **reading assignments** are approximately thirty pages each; some are a little shorter while others are a little longer. Students have approximately 15 minutes of pre-reading work to do prior to each reading assignment. This pre-reading work involves reviewing the study questions for the assignment and doing some vocabulary work for some challenging vocabulary words they will encounter in their reading.

The **study guide questions** are fact-based questions; students can find the answers to these questions right in the text. These questions come in two formats: short answer or multiple choice. The best use of these materials is probably to use the short answer version of the questions as study guides for students (since answers will be more complete), and to use the multiple choice version for occasional quizzes. It might be a good idea to make transparencies of your answer keys for the overhead projector.

The **vocabulary work** is intended to enrich students' vocabularies as well as to aid in the students' understanding of the play. Prior to each reading assignment, students will complete a two-part worksheet for approximately 10 vocabulary words in the upcoming reading assignment. Part I focuses on students' use of general knowledge and contextual clues by giving the sentence in which the word appears in the text. Students are then to write down what they think the words mean based on the words' usage. Part II nails down the definitions of the words by giving students dictionary definitions of the words and having students match the words to the correct definitions based on the words' contextual usage. Students should then have an understanding of the words when they meet them in the text.

After each reading assignment, students will go back and formulate answers for the study guide questions. Discussion of these questions serves as a **review** of the most important events and ideas presented in the reading assignments.

After students complete reading the work, there is a **vocabulary review** lesson which pulls together all of the fragmented vocabulary lists for the reading assignments and gives students a review of all of the words they have studied.

Following the vocabulary review, a lesson is devoted to the **extra discussion questions/writing assignments**. These questions focus on interpretation, critical analysis and personal response, employing a variety of thinking skills and adding to the students' understanding of the play.

The **group project** which follows the discussion questions has students working together to discuss the major themes and ideas in the play.

There are three **writing assignments** in this unit, each with the purpose of informing, persuading, or having students express personal opinions. The first assignment is to express personal opinions: students express their opinions about the importance of having some illusions in life, rather than seeing all of the realities of the world with no "buffer." The second assignment is to inform: students take the information they found through their nonfiction reading assignments and form it into a composition, in preparation for the oral presentation they will have to make. The third assignment is to persuade: students persuade their audience that *The Tempest* either is or is not Shakespeare's farewell to his audience.

In addition, there is a **nonfiction reading assignment**. Students are required to read a piece of nonfiction related in some way to *Tempest*. After reading their nonfiction pieces, students will fill out a worksheet on which they answer questions regarding facts, interpretation, criticism, and personal opinions. During one class period, students make **oral presentations** about the nonfiction pieces they have read. This not only exposes all students to a wealth of information, it also gives students the opportunity to practice **public speaking**. This nonfiction assignment is done in conjunction with the introductory research assignment.

The **review lesson** pulls together all of the aspects of the unit. The teacher is given four or five choices of activities or games to use which all serve the same basic function of reviewing all of the information presented in the unit.

The **unit tests** come in two formats: all multiple choice-matching-true/false or with a mixture of matching, short answer, multiple choice, and composition. As a convenience, two different tests for each format have been included. There is also an advanced short answer version of the unit test.

There are additional **support materials** included with this unit. The **resource sections** include suggestions for an in-class library, crossword and word search puzzles related to the play, and extra vocabulary worksheets. There is a list of **bulletin board ideas** which gives the teacher suggestions for bulletin boards to go along with this unit. In addition, there is a list of **extra class activities** the teacher could choose from to enhance the unit or as a substitution for an exercise the teacher might feel is inappropriate for his/her class. **Answer keys** are located directly after the **reproducible student materials** throughout the unit. The student materials may be reproduced for use in the teacher's classroom without infringement of copyrights. No other portion of this unit may be reproduced without the written consent of Teacher's Pet Publications, Inc.

UNIT OBJECTIVES - *Tempest*

1. Through reading Shakespeare's *Tempest* students will study the ideas of good coming from bad, atonement and reconciliation, purification through suffering, illusion versus reality, and nature versus society..

2. Students will demonstrate their understanding of the text on four levels: factual, interpretive, critical and personal.

3. Students will analyze characters to better understand motivation for action.

4. Students will have their oral reading evaluated.

5. Students will examine Shakespeare's use of language.

6. Students will be given the opportunity to practice reading aloud and silently to improve their skills in each area.

7. Students will answer questions to demonstrate their knowledge and understanding of the main events and characters in *Tempest* as they relate to the author's theme development.

8. Students will enrich their vocabularies and improve their understanding of the play through the vocabulary lessons prepared for use in conjunction with the play.

9. The writing assignments in this unit are geared to several purposes:
    a. To have students demonstrate their abilities to inform, to persuade, or to express their own personal ideas

        Note: Students will demonstrate ability to write effectively to <u>inform</u> by developing and organizing facts to convey information. Students will demonstrate the ability to write effectively to <u>persuade</u> by selecting and organizing relevant information, establishing an argumentative purpose, and by designing an appropriate strategy for an identified audience. Students will demonstrate the ability to write effectively to <u>express personal ideas</u> by selecting a form and its appropriate elements.

    b. To check the students' reading comprehension
    c. To make students think about the ideas presented by the play
    d. To encourage logical thinking
    e. To provide an opportunity to practice good grammar and improve students' use of the English language.

READING ASSIGNMENT SHEET - *Tempest*

Date Assigned	Reading Assignment Act: Scene(s)	Completion Date
	I	
	II	
	III	
	IV	
	V	

UNIT OUTLINE - *The Tempest*

1 Introduction	2 Practice Speaking Parts	3 Read Act I PV Act II	4 Study ?s Act I Read Act II PV Act III	5 Study ?s Act II Read Act III PV Act IV
6 Writing Assignment #1	7 Study ?s Act III Read Act IV PV Act V	8 Study ?s Act IV Read Act V Assign Extra ?s	9 Study ?s Act V Extra Discussion ?s	10 Vocabulary
11 Library	12 Writing Assignment #2	13 NFR Reports	14 Group Activity	15 Group Discussion
16 Writing Assignment #3	17 Review	18 Test		

Key: P = Preview Study Questions   V = Vocabulary Work   R = Read

STUDY GUIDE QUESTIONS

SHORT ANSWER STUDY GUIDE QUESTIONS - *The Tempest*

Act I
1. Why is the boatswain so rude to his passengers?
2. How did Prospero and Miranda come to live on the island?
3. Who is Caliban?
4. Who is Ferdinand, and what happens when he meets Miranda?
5. Why did Prospero become rude to Ferdinand?

Act II
1. What do Anthony and Sebastian do while the others sleep?
2. Why didn't Sebastian kill Alonso?
3. Why does Caliban take up with Stephano and Trinculo?

Act III
1. What do Ferdinand and Miranda decide to do in Scene One?
2. What does Caliban want to do with Stephano and Trinculo while Prospero naps in the afternoon? Why?
3. What tricks do Prospero and Ariel play on Alonso's group?
4. What is Alonso's reaction to Ariel's reminders? Sebastian's? Antonio's?

Act IV
1. What is Prospero's "gift" to Ferdinand?
2. For what purpose did Prospero produce spirits to play Iris, Ceres and Juno?
3. What tricks do Prospero and Ariel play on Caliban, Stephano, and Trinculo?

Act V
1. Why does Prospero release the king's group?
2. What is Prospero's reaction when Alonso tries to apologize to Miranda for sending her and her father away?
3. What is ironic about Miranda's "brave new world" lines?
4. How does Prospero force Sebastian and Antonio into the background?
5. How does Caliban react when back in Prospero's presence?
6. What is Prospero's final command to Ariel?

ANSWER KEY: SHORT ANSWER STUDY GUIDE QUESTIONS - *The Tempest*

Act I

1. Why is the boatswain so rude to his passengers?
   The ship is in a storm. The master and boatswain (and crew) are doing everything they can to keep the ship from going down. The royal passengers keep popping out from below and bothering the boatswain. Thus, instead of just not helping, they are actually causing additional problems. The boatswain just wants them to stay where they belong and to let him work.

2. How did Prospero and Miranda come to live on the island?
   Prospero's brother Antonio and Alonso, King of Naples, conspired and overthrew Prospero. Prospero and his daughter Miranda were cast out. Gonzalo, the nobleman assigned to set them off, felt sorry for them and packed their boat with provisions. Some time later their boat was cast upon the shore of the island.

3. Who is Caliban?
   He is the son of the bad witch Sycorax. Through his magic, Prospero has made Caliban, a deformed, bestial human, his slave. Prospero taught Caliban and treated him kindly until Caliban tried to rape Miranda. Since then, Caliban has grown resentful of rough treatment and Prospero's taking over the island.

4. Who is Ferdinand, and what happens when he meets Miranda?
   He is the son of the King of Naples. When Ferdinand and Miranda meet, they instantly fall in love.

5. Why did Prospero become rude to Ferdinand?
   "They [Ferdinand and Miranda] are both in either's powers. But this is swift business/I must uneasy make, lest too light winning/Make light the prize."

Act II

1. What do Anthony and Sebastian do while the others sleep?
   Anthony suggested that Sebastian should kill Alonso while he was sleeping. Sebastian said, "As thou got'st Milan,/I'll come by Naples. Draw thy sword."

2. Why didn't Sebastian kill Alonso?
   Ariel woke up Gonzalo and Alonso.

3. Why does Caliban take up with Stephano and Trinculo?
   He meets them in the woods and mistakes the drunken Stephano for a god. Thinking Stephano will be able to defeat Prospero, and being disenchanted with Prospero, he decides to side with Stephano.

Act III

1. What do Ferdinand and Miranda decide to do in Scene One?
   They decide to get married.

2. What does Caliban want to do with Stephano and Trinculo while Prospero naps in the afternoon? Why?
   He wants to kill Prospero while he sleeps so Stephano and Miranda can be King and Queen of the island with Caliban and Trinculo as lords.

3. What tricks do Prospero and Ariel play on Alonso's group?
   Prospero shows them a feast and then makes it disappear. Ariel reminds them of their sins, their injustices towards Prospero.

4. What is Alonso's reaction to Ariel's reminders? Sebastian's? Antonio's?
   Alonso feels bad, thinking that his son (Ferdinand) was killed as Heaven's way of making punishing him for his evil deeds. Sebastian and Alonso are ready to fight the "Fiends" who bring this message.

Act IV

1. What is Prospero's "gift" to Ferdinand?
   Miranda is his gift.

2. For what purpose did Prospero produce spirits to play Iris, Ceres and Juno?
   He produced them as entertainment to help celebrate the engagement of Ferdinand and Miranda.

3. What tricks do Prospero and Ariel play on Caliban, Stephano, and Trinculo?
   First Ariel leads them through briars and thorns and leaves them in a dirty pond. Then Prospero has Ariel put out "glistening" clothes for them (as bait). Finally, Prospero has spirits in the form of dogs chase the three away.

Act V

1. Why does Prospero release the king's group?
   When giving the report about the party's well-being, Ariel mentioned "That if you now beheld them, your [Prospero's] affections/Would become tender." Prospero later decides "The rarer action is/In virtue than in vengeance."

2. What is Prospero's reaction when Alonso tries to apologize to Miranda for sending her and her father away?
   Prospero says, "Let us not burden our remembrances with/A heaviness that's gone." In other words, he wants the past to be done and to start fresh.

3. What is ironic about Miranda's "brave new world" lines?
   The people she sees, whom she thinks represent a great humankind she has not known, are actually conspirators and would-be murderers.

4. How does Prospero force Sebastian and Antonio into the background?
   He lets them know he knows of their plot to kill Alonso and Gonzalo.

5. How does Caliban react when back in Prospero's presence?
　　He comes groveling back to Prospero when he realizes that Stephano has no power.

6. What is Prospero's final command to Ariel?
　　He commands Ariel to give them good seas and fair winds to send them home.

MULTIPLE CHOICE STUDY GUIDE/QUIZ QUESTIONS - *The Tempest*

Act I

1. Why is the boatswain so rude to his passengers?
    - A. He doesn't think they have paid enough, and he is angry (really at himself) because he took them anyway.
    - B. They have been rude to him, so he is treating them the same way.
    - C. He is drunk. He gets rude and boisterous whenever he drinks.
    - D. The ship is in a storm. The passengers keep bothering the crew while they are working, causing more problems.

2. How did Prospero and Miranda come to live on the island?
    - A. Prospero's brother Antonio and Alonso, the King of Naples, conspired and overthrew Prospero. Prospero and his daughter Miranda, were cast out. Gonzalo, the nobleman assigned to set them off, felt sorry for them and packed their boat with provisions. The boat was later cast upon the island.
    - B. Prospero felt it was time to retire and leave the work of governing to his son. His daughter, Miranda, offered to come to the island with him and help him get settled.
    - C. Miranda was being courted by a man she didn't want to marry. In order to protect her, her father took her to the island. At the same time, he had arranged for his soldiers to kill the suitor.
    - D. Prospero had contracted a mysterious degenerative disease. The doctors didn't know how to cure it. Fearing that he was contagious, they banned him from his homeland, and sent him to the island to live. His daughter, Miranda, went along to nurse him.

3. Which of the following statements does not describe Caliban?
    - A. He is the son of the bad witch Sycorax.
    - B. He is deformed and bestial-looking.
    - C. He is highly intelligent, although he doesn't show it.
    - D. He is Prospero's slave.

4. True or False: When Ferdinand and Miranda meet, they develop and instant dislike for each other.
    - A. True
    - B. False

5. Who says the following lines, and who is being spoken about? "They are both in either's powers. But this is swift business/ I must uneasy make, lest too light winning/Make light the prize."
    - A. Prospero is talking about Ferdinand and Miranda.
    - B. The King of Naples is talking about winning the war against Antonio.
    - C. Caliban is talking about Prospero and Ferdinand.
    - D. Miranda is talking about Ferdinand and Alonso.

Tempest Multiple Choice Study/Quiz Questions Page 2

Act II

6. What do Anthony and Sebastian do while the others sleep?
    A. They steal Prospero's fortune.
    B. They attack Miranda.
    C. They conspire with Caliban.
    D. They plot to kill Alonso.

7. Is their plan successful?
    A. Yes, it is.
    B. No, it isn't.

8. True or False: Caliban meets Stephano and Trinculo in the woods, and mistakes Stephano for a god. Thinking Stephano will be able to defeat Prospero, and being disenchanted with Prospero, he decides to side with Stephano.
    A. True
    B. False

Tempest Multiple Choice Study/Quiz Questions Page 3

<u>Act III</u>

9. What do Ferdinand and Miranda decide to do in Scene One?
   - A. They decide to kill Alonso.
   - B. They decide to get married.
   - C. They decide to steal a boat and leave the island.
   - D. They decide to force the others to have a peace talk.

10. What does Caliban want to do with Stephano and Trinculo while Prospero naps in the afternoon and why?
    - A. He wants to kidnap them and hold them for ransom so he can get rich.
    - B. He wants them to steal Prospero's money and a boat so they can get off the island.
    - C. He wants them to collect all of the driftwood, including the remains of the ship, so they can build a huge signal fire.
    - D. He wants to kill Prospero while he sleeps so Stephano and Miranda can be King and Queen of the island with Caliban and Trinculo as lords.

11. What tricks do Prospero and Ariel play on Alonso's group?
    - A. Prospero and Ariel make the members of the group think they all have animal heads.
    - B. Prospero makes them thing they can hear each other's thoughts. Ariel makes them fall in love with each other.
    - C. Prospero shows them a feast and then makes it disappear. Ariel reminds them of their sins, their injustices towards Prospero.
    - D. Prospero creates a huge storm and makes them think they are all going to drown. Ariel makes them selfish and unwilling to help each other.

12. Whose reaction is to feel bad, thinking that he is being punished for his evil deeds?
    - A. Sebastian
    - B. Ferdinand
    - C. Alonso
    - D. Caliban

Tempest Multiple Choice Study/Quiz Questions Page 4

Act IV

13. What is Prospero's gift to Ferdinand?
    A. Miranda is his gift.
    B. Prospero gives Ferdinand all of his vast wealth.
    C. Prospero gives him the island.
    D. He gives him eternal youth.

14. For what purpose did Prospero produce the spirits to play Iris, Ceres, and Juno?
    A. He wanted to scare the others into leaving him alone.
    B. He needed help to get rid of his tormentors.
    C. He wanted them to entertain at a celebration he had planned.
    D. He wanted them to protect Miranda from the evil men on the island.

15. Which is not one of the tricks that Prospero and Ariel play on Caliban?
    A. The three think they are eating succulent fruit, but it changes to worms as they begin to bite into it.
    B. They are lead through briars and thorns and left in a dirty pond.
    C. Ariel puts on "glistening" clothes as bait.
    D. Spirits in the form of dogs chase the three away.

Tempest Multiple Choice Study/Quiz Questions Page 5

Act V

16. What are Prospero and Ariel talking about in the following quotes: "That if you now beheld them, your affections/Would become tender." "The rarer action is/In virtue than in vengeance."
    A. Ariel thinks Prospero should let Miranda make her own decisions.
    B. Ariel thinks Prospero should release the king's group.

17. Who says "Let us not burden our remembrances with/A heaviness that's gone."?
    A. Ariel says it.
    B. Miranda says it.
    C. Alonso says it.
    D. Prospero says it.

18. What is ironic about Miranda's "brave new world" lines?
    A. She is not really brave at all.
    B. The people that she thinks represent a great humankind are really conspirators and would-be murderers.
    C. She doesn't know that her father said the same thing twenty years earlier.
    D. The explorers of the times are really on the verge of discovering "the New World"

19. How does Prospero force Sebastian and Antonio into the background?
    A. He pays them each a small pouch of gold and jewels.
    B. He offers to teach them some of his magic.
    C. He lets them know he knows of their plot to kill Alonso and Gonzalo.
    D. He offers to find wives for them.

20. How does Caliban react when back in Prospero's presence?
    A. He comes groveling back to Prospero when he realizes that Stephano has not power.
    B. He is pleased with his new-found independence. He maintains his distance and his dignity.

21. What is Prospero's final command to Ariel?
    A. He commands her to make sure everyone is happy.
    B. He commands her to make sure they are well fed.
    C. He commands her to erase all memories of recent events from their minds.
    D. He commands her to give them good seas and fair winds to send them home.

ANSWER KEY - MULTIPLE CHOICE STUDY/QUIZ QUESTIONS
The Tempest

Act I	Act II	Act III	Act IV	Act V
1. D.	6. D	9. B	13. A	16. B
2. A.	7. B	10. D	14. C	17. D
3. C.	8. A	11. C	15. A	18. B
4. B.				19. C
5. A.				20. A
				21. D

PREREADING VOCABULARY WORKSHEETS

VOCABULARY - *The Tempest*

<u>Act I</u> Part I: Using Prior Knowledge and Contextual Clues

    Below are the sentences in which the vocabulary words appear in the text. Read the sentence. Use any clues you can find in the sentence combined with your prior knowledge, and write what you think the underlined words mean in the space provided.

1. A pox o' your throat, you bawling, <u>blasphemous</u>, incharitable dog!

2. Hang, you whoreson, <u>insolent</u> noisemaker!

3. I have such provision in mine art
   So safely ordered that there is no soul,
   No, not so much <u>perdition</u> as a hair
   Betid to any creature in the vessel

4. I pray thee mark me -- that a brother should
   Be so <u>perfidious</u>! --

5. As my trust was, which had indeed no limit,
   A confidence <u>sans</u> bound.

6. <u>Abhorred</u> slave!

7.   I <u>endowed</u> thy purposes
   With words that made them known.

8. This music crept by me upon the waters,
   <u>Allaying</u> both their fury and my passion
   With its sweet air.

Tempest Prereading Vocabulary Worksheet Act I Continued

9.   Myself am Naples,
   Who with mine eyes, never since at <u>ebb</u>, beheld
   The King my father wrecked.

10.   Thou dost here <u>usurp</u>
   The name thou owest not, and hast put thyself
   Upon this island as a spy, to win it
   From me, the lord on 't.

Act I - Part II: Determining the Meaning

   You have tried to figure out the meanings of the vocabulary words for Act One. Now match the vocabulary words to their dictionary definitions. If there are words for which you cannot figure out the definition by contextual clues and by process of elimination, look them up in a dictionary.

___ 1. blasphemous   A. insulting in manner; rude; impertinent
___ 2. insolent   B. equipped; supplied
___ 3. perdition   C. decline; flowing away
___ 4. perfidious   D. irreverent
___ 5. sans   E. abominable; loathsome
___ 6. abhorred   F. treacherous
___ 7. endowed   G. take over without legal authority
___ 8. allaying   H. utter ruin; eternal damnation
___ 9. ebb   I. calming; relieving
___10. usurp   J. without

Vocabulary - *The Tempest* Act II

Part I: Using Prior Knowledge and Contextual Clues

Below are the sentences in which the vocabulary words appear in the text. Read the sentence. Use any clues you can find in the sentence combined with your prior knowledge, and write what you think the underlined words mean in the space provided.

1. Dolor comes to him, indeed. You have spoken truer than you purposed.

2. It must needs be of subtle, tender, and delicate temperance.

3.   He trod the water,
   Whose enmity he flung aside, and breasted
   The surge most swoln that met him.

4. Do not omit the heavy offer of it.

5.   There be that can rule Naples
   As well as he that sleeps, lords that can prate
   As amply and unnecessarily
   As this Gonzalo.

6. This is a scurvy tune too, but here's my comfort.

Tempest Prereading Vocabulary Act II Continued

Act II - Part II: Determining the Meaning

You have tried to figure out the meanings of the vocabulary words for Act Two. Now match the vocabulary words to their dictionary definitions. If there are words for which you cannot figure out the definition by contextual clues and by process of elimination, look them up in a dictionary.

___ 1. dolor   A. chatter
___ 2. subtle   B. contemptible
___ 3. enmity   C. slight; difficult to detect
___ 4. omit   D. deep hatred
___ 5. prate   E. grief; sorrow
___ 6. scurvy   F. leave out

Vocabulary - *The Tempest* <u>Act III</u>

Part I: Using Prior Knowledge and Contextual Clues

Below are the sentences in which the vocabulary words appear in the text. Read the sentence. Use any clues you can find in the sentence combined with your prior knowledge, and write what you think the underlined words mean in the space provided.

1. This my mean task
   Would be as heavy to me and as <u>odious</u>, but
   The mistress which I serve quickens what's dead
   And makes my labors pleasures.

2. Full many a lady
   I have eyed with best regard, and many a time
   The harmony of their tongues hath into bondage
   Brought my too <u>diligent</u> ear.

3. But I prattle
   Something too wildly, and my father's <u>precepts</u>
   I therin do forget.

4. For now thy are oppressed with travel, they
   Will not, nor cannot, use such <u>vigilance</u>
   As when they are fresh.

5. You are three men of sin, whom Destiny --
   That hath to instrument this lower world
   And what is in 't -- the never-<u>surfeited</u> sea
   Hath caused to belch up you.

6. My fellow ministers
   Are like <u>invulnerable</u>. If you could hurt,
   Your swords are now too massy for your strengths,
   And will not be uplifted.

7. But remember --
   For that's my business to you -- that you three
   From Milan did <u>supplant</u> good Prospero,

Tempest Prereading Vocabulary Act III Continued

Act III - Part II: Determining the Meaning

    You have tried to figure out the meanings of the vocabulary words for Act III. Now match the vocabulary words to their dictionary definitions. If there are words for which you cannot figure out the definition by contextual clues and by process of elimination, look them up in a dictionary.

___ 1. odious   A. watchfulness
___ 2. diligent   B. rules; principles
___ 3. precepts   C. displace and substitute
___ 4. vigilance   D. overfilled
___ 5. surfeited   E. arousing strong dislike or displeasure
___ 6. invulnerable   F. unable to be damaged; impenetrable
___ 7. supplant   G. marked by perseverance

Vocabulary - *The Tempest* Act IV

Part I: Using Prior Knowledge and Contextual Clues
　　Below are the sentences in which the vocabulary words appear in the text. Read the sentence. Use any clues you can find in the sentence combined with your prior knowledge, and write what you think the underlined words mean in the space provided.

1. If I have too austerely punished you,
　Your compensation makes amends.

2. 　　All thy vexations
　Were but my trials of thy love

3-4. 　　But
　If thou dost break her virgin knot before
　All sanctimonious ceremonies may
　With full and holy rite be ministered,
　 No sweet aspersion shall the Heavens let fall
　To make this contract grow; but barren hate,
　Sour-eyed disdain and discord shall bestrew
　The union of your bed . . . .

5. 　　I warrant you, sir,
　The white cold virgin snow upon my heart
　Abates the ardor of my liver.

6. 　　Here thought they to have done
　Some wanton charm upon this man and maid,

Tempest Prereading Vocabulary Worksheet Act IV continued

7.   I had forgot that foul conspiracy
   Of the beast Caliban and his <u>confederates</u>
   Against my life.

8.   Sir, I am <u>vexed</u>.
   Bear with my weakness, my old brain is troubled.

9.   Then I beat my <u>tabor</u>.

Act IV - Part II: Determining the Meaning

You have tried to figure out the meanings of the vocabulary words for Act IV. Now match the vocabulary words to their dictionary definitions. If there are words for which you cannot figure out the definition by contextual clues and by process of elimination, look them up in a dictionary.

___ 1. austerely   A. contempt; scorn
___ 2. vexations   B. troubled; annoyed; bothered
___ 3. sanctimonious   C. severely
___ 4. disdain   D. lewd; excessive
___ 5. ardor   E. annoyances; troubles
___ 6. wanton   F. allies; comrades; accomplices
___ 7. confederates   G. a small drum
___ 8. vexed   H. religious
___ 9. tabor   I. fiery intensity; strong enthusiasm

Vocabulary - *The Tempest* Act V

Part I: Using Prior Knowledge and Contextual Clues
    Below are the sentences in which the vocabulary words appear in the text. Read the sentence. Use any clues you can find in the sentence combined with your prior knowledge, and write what you think the underlined words mean in the space provided.

1.   They being penitent,
   The sole drift of my purpose doth extend
   Not a frown further.

2.   The strong-based promontory
   Have I made shake, and by the spurs plucked up
   The pine and cedar.

3.   But this rough magic
   I here abjure, and when I have required
   Some heavenly music --- which even now I do --
   To work mine end upon their senses, that
   This airy charm is for, I'll break my staff,

4. Irreparable is the loss, and Patience
   Says it is past her cure.

5.   Some oracle
   Must rectify our knowledge.

6-7.   I'll deliver all,
   And promise you calm seas, auspicious gales,
   And sail so expeditious that shall catch
   Your royal fleet far off.

39

Tempest Prereading Vocabulary Worksheet Act V Continued

Act V - Part II: Determining the Meaning

You have tried to figure out the meanings of the vocabulary words for Act V. Now match the vocabulary words to their dictionary definitions. If there are words for which you cannot figure out the definition by contextual clues and by process of elimination, look them up in a dictionary.

___ 1. penitent A. give up; forswear
___ 2. promontory B. favorable
___ 3. abjure C. unable to be fixed
___ 4. irreparable D. done with speed and efficiency
___ 5. oracle E. remorseful; sorry
___ 6. auspicious F. a high ridge of rock jutting into the water
___ 7. expeditious G. a wise person or source of wisdom

ANSWER KEY - VOCABULARY
The Tempest

Act I
1. D
2. A
3. H
4. F
5. J
6. E
7. B
8. I
9. C
10. G

Act II
1. E
2. C
3. D
4. F
5. A
6. B

Act III
1. E
2. G
3. B
4. A
5. D
6. F
7. C

Act IV
1. C
2. E
3. H
4. A
5. I
6. D
7. F
8. B
9. G

Act V
1. E
2. F
3. A
4. C
5. G
6. B
7. D

DAILY LESSONS

LESSON ONE

Objectives
1. To introduce the theme of illusion versus reality
2. To distribute the materials which will be used in the unit
3. To assign the speaking parts for the reading of the play

NOTE: Prior to this lesson you need to have invited an illusionist/magician or have acquired a video illustrating several illusions performed by an illusionist/magician. If you cannot arrange for either of these, have students bring in things that represent optical or other kinds of illusions, and use your class time exploring the things students have brought in.

Activity #1
Spend the first half of your class time looking at and/or discussing various illusions to introduce the theme of illusion versus reality. After this activity, explain to students that the play they are about to read has the theme of illusion versus reality shown in many ways -- that they should look for this theme as they read.

Activity #2
Distribute the materials which will be used in this unit. Explain in detail how students are to use these materials.

Study Guides Students should read the study guide questions for each reading assignment prior to beginning the reading assignment to get a feeling for what events and ideas are important in the section they are about to read. After reading the section, students will (as a class or individually) answer the questions to review the important events and ideas from that section of the play. Students should keep the study guides as study materials for the unit test.

Vocabulary Prior to reading a reading assignment, students will do vocabulary work related to the section of the play they are about to read. Following the completion of the reading of the play, there will be a vocabulary review of all the words used in the vocabulary assignments. Students should keep their vocabulary work as study materials for the unit test.

Reading Assignment Sheet You need to fill in the reading assignment sheet to let students know by when their reading has to be completed. You can either write the assignment sheet up on a side blackboard or bulletin board and leave it there for students to see each day, or you can "ditto" copies for each student to have. In either case, you should advise students to become very familiar with the reading assignments so they know what is expected.

Extra Activities Center The Unit Resources portion of this unit contains suggestions for an extra library of related plays and articles in your classroom as well as crossword and word search puzzles. Make an extra activities center in your room where you will keep these materials for students to use. (Bring the books and articles in from the library and keep several copies of the puzzles on hand.) Explain to students that these materials are available for students to use when they finish reading assignments or other class work early.

Nonfiction Assignment Sheet Explain to students that they each are to read at least one non-fiction piece from the in-class library at some time during the unit. Students will fill out a nonfiction assignment sheet after completing the reading to help you (the teacher) evaluate their reading experiences and to help the students think about and evaluate their own reading experiences.

Books Each school has its own rules and regulations regarding student use of school books. Advise students of the procedures that are normal for your school.

Activity #3
Distribute the Speaking Parts Assignment Sheet. Explain to students that the play will be read orally. Each student will be responsible for reading a particular part (or parts) as noted on the assignment sheet.

Activity #4
Explain to students that prior to Lesson Three they should have previewed the study questions and should have also completed the prereading vocabulary worksheet for Act I. Show students how to do these two activities.

LESSON TWO

Objective
To help prepare students for their oral reading of the play

Activity
Give students this class period to rehearse their speaking parts for the play. Have students get together in groups for each scene and rehearse their lines. Advise students that their oral reading will be graded.

SPEAKING PART ASSIGNMENTS
The Tempest

A:S	PART	ASSIGNED TO	A:S	PART	ASSIGNED TO
I:I	NARRATOR		III:II	GONZALO	
	BOATSWAIN			ALONSO	
	ALONSO			ANTONIO	
	ANTONIO			SEBASTIAN	
	GONZALO			PROSPERO	
	SEBASTIAN			ARIEL	
	MARINERS/SJO[,ASTER		IV	NARRATOR	
I:II	NARRATOR			PROSPERO	
	MIRANDA			FERDINAND	
	PROSPERO			ARIEL	
	ARIEL			IRIS	
	CLAIBAN			CERTES	
	FERDINAND			JUNO	
II:I	NARRATOR			MIRANDA	
	GONZALO			CALIBAN	
	ALONSO			TRINCULO	
	SEBASTIAN			STEPHANO	
	ANTONIO		V	NARRATOR	
	ARIEL			PROSPERO	
II:II	NARRATOR			ARIEL	
	CALIBAN			GONZALO	
	STEPHANO			SEBASTIAN	
	TRINCULO			STEPHANO	
III:I	NARRATOR			TRINCULO	
	FERDINAND			BOATSWAIN	
	MIRANDA			FERDINAND	
	PROSPERO			MIRANDA	
III:II	NARRATOR			CALIBAN	
	STEPHANO				
	TRINCULO				
	CALIBAN				

47

NONFICTION ASSIGNMENT SHEET - *The Tempest*
(To be completed after reading the required nonfiction article)

Name _____ Date _____

Title of Nonfiction Read _____

Written By _____ Publication Date _____

I. Factual Summary: Write a short summary of the piece you read.

II. Vocabulary
    1. With which vocabulary words in the piece did you encounter some degree of difficulty?

    2. How did you resolve your lack of understanding with these words?

III. Interpretation: What was the main point the author wanted you to get from reading his work?

IV. Criticism
    1. With which points of the piece did you agree or find easy to accept? Why?

    2. With which points of the piece did you disagree or find difficult to believe? Why?

V. Personal Response: What do you think about this piece? OR How does this piece influence your ideas?

LESSON THREE

Objectives
> 1. To read Act I
> 2. To do the prereading activities for Act II

NOTE: Since the level of your class and your students' reading abilities will determine the amount of time needed for each act, just use these lessons as a guideline. If you do not finish Act I in this class period, for example, carry it over into the next class period.

Activity #1

Explain that because *Tempest* is a play it is meant to be acted on a stage. If you are not planning a production of the play, explain to students that the next best thing we can do is to read the parts orally. Each person in class will (eventually) have a speaking part to perform. The part does not have to be memorized, but the students' oral reading will be evaluated.

Have students who were assigned to read parts for Act I do so during this class period. If you have not yet evaluated students' oral reading this marking period, this would be a good opportunity to do so. An Oral Reading Evaluation form is included in this unit for your convenience.

Activity #2

Tell students that prior to your next class meeting they should have previewed the study questions and have completed the prereading vocabulary worksheet for Act II.

LESSON FOUR

Objectives
    1. To review the main events and ideas presented in Act I
    2. To read Act II
    3. To do the prereading work for Act III

Activity #1

    Give students a few minutes to formulate answers for the study guide questions for Act I, and then discuss the answers to the questions in detail. Write the answers on the board or overhead transparency so students can have the correct answers for study purposes. Note: It is a good practice in public speaking and leadership skills for individual students to take charge of leading the discussions of the study questions. Perhaps a different student could go to the front of the class and lead the discussion each day that the study questions are discussed during this unit. Of course, the teacher should guide the discussion when appropriate and be sure to fill in any gaps the students leave.

Activity #2

    Have students read Act II orally in class. Continue the oral reading evaluations.

Activity #3

    Prior to reading Act II, students should preview the study questions and do the prereading vocabulary work for Act II. Give students the remainder of this class period to do the prereading work and, if they finish that, to begin practicing their oral reading parts.

ORAL READING EVALUATION - *The Tempest*

Name _____ Class _____ Date _____

SKILL	EXCELLENT	GOOD	AVERAGE	FAIR	POOR
Fluency	5	4	3	2	1
Clarity	5	4	3	2	1
Audibility	5	4	3	2	1
Pronunciation	5	4	3	2	1
_____	5	4	3	2	1
_____	5	4	3	2	1

Total _____ Grade _____

Comments:

LESSON FIVE

Objectives
1. To review the main ideas and events from Act II
2. To read Act III of *The Tempest*
3. To evaluate students' oral reading
4. To do the prereading work for Act IV

Activity #1
Give students a few minutes to formulate answers for the study guide questions for Act II, and then discuss the answers to the questions in detail. Write the answers on the board or overhead transparency so students can have the correct answers for study purposes.

Activity #2
Have students who were assigned to read parts for Act II do so during this class period. Continue the oral reading evaluations.

Activity #4
Tell students that they should preview the study questions for Act IV and complete the prereading vocabulary worksheet for Act IV prior to Lesson Seven. (Give students the day/date.)

LESSON SIX

Objectives
1. To give students practice writing their own opinions
2. To further examine the idea of illusions in life
3. To give the teacher the opportunity to evaluate students' writing

Activity
Distribute Writing Assignment 1. Discuss the directions in detail and give students this class period to do the assignment.

Follow - Up: After you have graded the assignments, have a writing conference with the students. After the writing conference, allow students to revise their papers using your suggestions and corrections. Give them about three days from the date they receive their papers to complete the revision. I suggest grading the revisions on an A-C-E scale (all revisions well-done, some revisions made, few or no revisions made). This will speed your grading time and still give some credit for the students' efforts.

WRITING ASSIGNMENT #1 - *Tempest*

PROMPT

In many of Shakespeare's plays, including *The Tempest*, the younger generation comes along to redeem the older generation -- or to show that there is hope for the future. Often the older generation (parents) will fight -- even to death -- but the son and daughter will fall in love and marry, ending the family feud. There is often the notion that the young people are more simple, more natural, less corrupted than those who have lived longer.

In similar terms, we often think of young people as being naive or having illusions about the world whereas older people are often described as disillusioned. A prime modern example of this idea is that many children believe in Santa Claus; they are under the illusion that Santa Claus exists and will bring them fabulous presents for Christmas morning. As they get older, they realize that there is no Santa Claus. As they get even older and have children, not only is there no Santa Claus to bring presents, but the full reality of the situation hits them -- *they* are Santa and have to face the reality of the shopping malls and the bills to be paid. For many people, the joy of Christmas they experienced as children becomes lost, and Christmas becomes a dreaded time of year. They become completely disillusioned.

Some people say that ignorance is bliss. Maybe ignorance creates or maintains illusions. Perhaps some illusions are necessary in life. With everything in life stripped to the bare reality, perhaps we would all be too disillusioned and would feel hopeless. Just imagine. If we knew every reality -- what all the politicians and corporate giants and the media and everyone were *really* doing. How would the world look to us? Think of the hullabaloo the various scandals that are exposed by the media cause. Suppose everything were exposed to us all the time?

Your assignment is to write a composition in which you give your opinions about the value -- or detriment -- of having illusions in life.

PREWRITING

The first thing to do is to stop and think about what you just read. What *do* you think? Write down the ideas that come to your mind on the topic. Just kind of brainstorm about the topic and jot down your thoughts. Take a look at what you've jotted down. Look for related ideas. Try to ascertain which ideas are the most important to you. Which things best express what you think about this topic? Gather your thoughts together and organize them in a logical way so that you can explain what you think.

DRAFTING

First write a paragraph in which you introduce the topic of your composition. The paragraphs in the body of your composition will all support or explain your main topic. The paragraphs should flow from idea to idea. Your final paragraph should include the conclusions you can draw from the information presented and should bring your composition to a close.

PROMPT

When you finish the rough draft of your paper, ask a student who sits near you to read it. After reading your rough draft, he/she should tell you what he/she liked best about your work, which parts were difficult to understand, and ways in which your work could be improved. Reread your paper considering your critic's comments, and make the corrections you think are necessary.

Do a final proofreading of your paper double-checking your grammar, spelling, organization, and the clarity of your ideas.

LESSON SEVEN

Objectives
  1. To review the main events and ideas presented in Act III
  2. To read Act IV
  3. To do the prereading work for Act III

Activity #1
  Give students a few minutes to formulate answers for the study guide questions for Act III, and then discuss the answers to the questions in detail. Write the answers on the board or overhead transparency so students can have the correct answers for study purposes.

Activity #2
  Have students read their speaking parts for Act IV of *The Tempest*. Continue the oral reading evaluations.

Activity #3
  Students should preview the study questions and do the prereading vocabulary work for Act V prior to your next class meeting.

LESSON EIGHT

Objectives
  1. To review the main events and ideas presented in Act IV
  2. To read Act V

Activity #1
  Give students a few minutes to formulate answers for the study guide questions for Act IV, and then discuss the answers to the questions in detail. Write the answers on the board or overhead transparency so students can have the correct answers for study purposes.

Activity #2
  Have students read their speaking parts for Act V of *The Tempest*. Continue the oral reading evaluations.

LESSON NINE

Objectives
1. To review the main ideas and events from Act V
2. To discuss *Tempest* on interpretive and critical levels

Activity #1
Give students a few minutes to formulate answers for the study guide questions for Act V, and then discuss the answers to the questions in detail.

Activity #2
Choose the questions from the Extra Discussion Questions/Writing Assignments which seem most appropriate for your students. A class discussion of these questions is most effective if students have been given the opportunity to formulate answers to the questions prior to the discussion. To this end, you may either have all the students formulate answers to all the questions, divide your class into groups and assign one or more questions to each group, or you could assign one question to each student in your class. The option you choose will make a difference in the amount of class time needed for this activity.

After students have had ample time to formulate answers to the questions, begin your class discussion of the questions and the ideas presented by the questions. Be sure students take notes during the discussion so they have information to study for the unit test.

EXTRA WRITING ASSIGNMENTS/DISCUSSION QUESTIONS - *Tempest*

Interpretation

1. Identify all the illusions to in the play.

2. What is the setting of *Tempest*?

3. Where is the climax of the play? Explain your choice.

4. Think of a different title for the play. Explain your choice.

5. What are the main conflicts in the play, and how are they resolved?

Critical

6. Explain how Shakespeare uses Ariel in the play and the effect of Ariel on the play.

7. Characterize William Shakespeare's style of writing. How does it contribute to the value of the play?

8. Are the characters' actions believably motivated? Why or why not?

9. Choose a passage from *The Tempest* (at least 10 lines). Analyze the meter, rhymes and word choice in relationship to the meaning and action of the passage.

10. Define "tragedy," "comedy," and "romance" in the theatrical/literary senses of the words and explain into what category or categories *The Tempest* falls.

11. What things in *The Tempest* are due to supernatural powers, and what effect does that have on our perception of the play?

12. Explain the idea of innocence versus experience as it relates to the play.

13. Compare and contrast Caliban and Ariel.

14. After the shipwreck, the passengers become separated into groups on the island. Compare and contrast the experiences of the groups: 1.) Alonso, Sebastian and Antonio 2.) Ferdinand 3.) Stephano and Trinculo.

Tempest Extra Discussion Questions page 2

15. What is Caliban's role in the play? What is the significance of his name? His physical characteristics?

16. Explain Caliban's relationship to Prospero in the play, both literally and symbolically/thematically.

17. Although Caliban is called "bestial," he often appears superior to Stephano and Trinculo. Explain this using examples from the play.

18. Trace Alonso's character development through the play.

Critical/Personal Response

19. What points does Shakespeare make about human nature in *The Tempest*?

20. Suppose Ferdinand and Miranda had not fallen in love immediately. How would that have changed the play?

21. What possible meanings could one derive from the Epilogue considering that this was one of the last plays Shakespeare wrote?

Personal Response

22. Did you enjoy reading *Tempest*? Why or why not?

23. Do you believe in "love at first sight"? Why or why not?

24. Have you read any other stories with characters like any of the characters in *The Tempest*? If so, describe how they were alike.

LESSON TEN

Objective

To review all the vocabulary words previewed in the play.

Activity

Choose one (or more) of the vocabulary review activities listed on the next page and spend your class period as directed in the activity. Some of the materials for these review activities are located in the Vocabulary Resource section of this unit.

LESSON ELEVEN

Objectives
1. To have students practice their researching skills
2. To give students practice using the resources of the library/media center
3. To have students learn about nonfiction topics related to the play

Activity

Take students to the library/media center. Tell students that they are each to read at least two articles about a nonfiction topic related to *The Tempest*. Some suggested topics are:

1. Ships and ship building
2. Sailing
3. Exploration -- particularly in the years 1600-1900
4. Elizabethan drama
5. History of mythology
6. Survival techniques
7. Any of the natives European explorers found in their travels
8. Milan or Naples
9. Illusions
10. The use of fairies or gods or goddesses in literature
11. Articles of criticism about *The Tempest*
12. French philosopher Montaigne's essay "Of Cannibals"

There are many more topics that could be used; these are just few suggestions.

Remind students to fill out Nonfiction Assignment Sheets for each article they read.

LESSON TWELVE

Objectives

    1. To give students the opportunity to practice writing to inform
    2. To give the teacher the opportunity to evaluate students' writing skills
    3. To help prepare students for their nonfiction reports

Activity #1

    Tell students that in the next class period they will have to give an oral report in which they share with the class the contents of the articles they have read. To help them prepare for this oral report, they should complete Writing Assignment #2.

Activity #2

    Distribute Writing Assignment #2. Discuss the directions in detail and give students ample time to complete the assignment.

LESSON THIRTEEN

Objectives

    1. To expose all students to a wealth of information about nonfiction topics related to *The Tempest*
    2. To give students practice speaking in front of a group of people
    3. To evaluate students' nonfiction reading work

Activity

    Ask each student to give a brief oral report about the nonfiction work he/she read for the research project assignment. Your criteria for evaluating this report will vary depending on the level of your students. You may wish for students to give a complete report without using notes of any kind, or you may want students to read directly from a written report, or you may want to do something in between these two extremes. Just make students aware of your criteria in ample time for them to prepare their reports.

VOCABULARY REVIEW ACTIVITIES - *The Tempest*

1. Divide your class into two teams and have an old-fashioned spelling or definition bee.

2. Give each of your students (or students in groups of two, three or four) *The Tempest* Vocabulary Word Search Puzzle. The person (group) to find all of the vocabulary words in the puzzle first wins.

3. Give students *The Tempest* Vocabulary Word Search Puzzle without the word list. The person or group to find the most vocabulary words in the puzzle wins.

4. Use *The Tempest* Vocabulary Crossword Puzzle. Put the puzzle onto a transparency on the overhead projector (so everyone can see it), and do the puzzle together as a class.

5. Give students *The Tempest* Vocabulary Matching Worksheet to do.

6. Divide your class into two teams. Use the *Tempest* vocabulary words with their letters jumbled as a word list. Student 1 from Team A faces off against Student 1 from Team B. You write the first jumbled word on the board. The first student (1A or 1B) to unscramble the word wins the chance for his/her team to score points. If 1A wins the jumble, go to student 2A and give him/her a definition. He/she must give you the correct spelling of the vocabulary word which fits that definition. If he/she does, Team A scores a point, and you give student 3A a definition for which you expect a correctly spelled matching vocabulary word. Continue giving Team A definitions until some team member makes an incorrect response. An incorrect response sends the game back to the jumbled-word face off, this time with students 2A and 2B. Instead of repeating giving definitions to the first few students of each team, continue with the student after the one who gave the last incorrect response on the team. For example, if Team B wins the jumbled-word face-off, and student 5B gave the last incorrect answer for Team B, you would start this round of definition questions with student 6B, and so on. The team with the most points wins!

7. Have students write a story in which they correctly use as many vocabulary words as possible. Have students read their compositions orally! Post the most original compositions on your bulletin board!

WRITING ASSIGNMENT #2
Tempest

PROMPT

When we read a story (in this case, a play) we bring to our reading our own knowledge and experiences to draw on as we read the story. For instance, when we say "stranded on an island," each of us draws upon an image -- a preconceived idea of what that means. Sometimes a story will suggest topics or ideas about which we do not have much prior knowledge or experience. In these cases, it is worthwhile to go back and read in more depth about these topics after reading the story in which the ideas were suggested. This not only adds to our own understanding of the story we have just read; it also gives us a bigger base of knowledge to take to our next reading experience and increases our understanding of our world. That is what the nonfiction reading assignment is meant to do.

All of you have read in more detail about topics related to *The Tempest*. Since we have the advantage of being together as a class, we can share our extra reading experiences and learn about many different topics without doing all of the reading and research ourselves. So, in the next class period, you will be asked to give an oral presentation about the nonfiction reading you have done. In this writing assignment you will make a written version of the oral presentation you will give. This will help organize and prepare you for your presentation.

PREWRITING

Most of your prewriting has been done through your reading and completion of the Nonfiction Assignment Sheets. Look at your nonfiction assignment sheets. Your information is already organized on these sheets. You have the bibliographical information about the article, the factual contents of the article, and your own critique of the article. That is all that is necessary for your presentation.

DRAFTING

Write a paragraph in which you introduce your topic and the bibliographic information about the two articles you read.

In the body of your composition write two paragraphs: one paragraph in which you give the facts from your first article, and one paragraph in which you give the facts from your second article.

Write a final paragraph in which you critique the two articles you read.

PROMPT

When you finish the rough draft of your paper, ask a student who sits near you to read it. After reading your rough draft, he/she should tell you what he/she liked best about your work, which parts were difficult to understand, and ways in which your work could be improved. Reread your paper considering your critic's comments, and make the corrections you think are necessary.

PROOFREADING

Do a final proofreading of your paper double-checking your grammar, spelling, organization, and the clarity of your ideas.

LESSONS FOURTEEN AND FIFTEEN

Objectives
1. To study the play more closely through all five acts
2. To give students the opportunity to practice their personal interaction skills in a small group setting
3. To give students the opportunity to practice their public speaking skills as they report their small group findings

Activity #1
Divide the class into groups. Each group should be assigned one of the following topics:
1. Good from Bad
2. Atonement and Reconciliation
3. Purification through Suffering
4. Nature vs. Society (Civilization)
5. Illusion vs. Reality

Each group should look at its topic through the entire play, and prepare to "teach" that topic to the class. Group members should divide the work into acts, giving each person of the group a specific act to research. After each member has had time to complete his research, the group members should share their findings with each other. They should then have a small discussion to try to draw any reasonable conclusions they can from the data they collected.

One group member should be designated "secretary" to jot down the group's ideas. Another should be designated "spokesperson" to report the group's ideas to the class.

Activity #2
The groups will each report their findings and conclusions to the whole class. The teacher or a student should write down on the board or overhead all of the findings and conclusions. Students should all take notes from the board for later study.

LESSON SIXTEEN

Objectives
    1. To give students the opportunity to practice writing to persuade
    2. To give the teacher the opportunity to evaluate students' writing skills
    3.

Activity #1

    Distribute Writing Assignment #3. Discuss the directions in detail and give students ample time to complete the assignment.

Activity #2

    While students are working on Writing Assignment #3, call individual students to your desk or some other private area for individual writing evaluation conferences based on the first two writing assignments. An evaluation form is included with this unit for your convenience.

LESSON SEVENTEEN

Objective
    To review the main ideas presented in *Tempest*

Activity #1

    Choose one of the review games/activities included in the packet and spend your class period as outlined there. Some materials for these activities are located in the Extra Activities Packet section of this unit.

Activity #2

    Remind students that the Unit Test will be in the next class meeting. Stress the review of the Study Guides and their class notes as a last minute, brush-up review for homework.

WRITING EVALUATION FORM - *Tempest*

Name _____ Date _____

Grade _____

Circle One For Each Item:

Grammar: correct   errors noted on paper

Spelling: correct   errors noted on paper

Punctuation: correct   errors noted on paper

Legibility: excellent   good   fair   poor

Strengths:

Weaknesses:

Comments/Suggestions:

WRITING ASSIGNMENT #3
The Tempest

PROMPT

About *The Tempest* L. L. Hillegas wrote,

"One widely-held view of the play is that it is Shakespeare's farewell to the stage; that in it he indicates to his audience that he will no longer write for them; that he has woven some part of many of his former plays into the fabric of this his last; and that the character of Prospero is biographical. Evidence for this theory is found in many of Prospero's speeches. In the final act of the play, for example, Prospero declares in a soliloquy that he will cast away his books and staff and deal in magic no more. Symbolically, Shakespeare is thought to be saying that he will lay aside his pen and no longer create magic (his poetry) for the stage. In the epilogue there is also some support for this interpretation. Shakespeare, in the person of Prospero, asks his audience to express approval of his works and release him from his servitude to them."

Your assignment is to write a composition in which you persuade your audience that *The Tempest* was, in fact, Shakespeare's farewell to the stage OR that it was *not* his last farewell to the stage.

PREWRITING

First, decide if you believe that *The Tempest* was Shakespeare's farewell. If you believe it was, write down several reasons *why* you believe it was. Your reasons should focus on the text, showing evidence supporting your belief. Write down examples using line references to note the portions of the text you intend to use as support.

If you decide *The Tempest* is not Shakespeare's farewell, give your reasons for that point of view, possibly using arguments to discredit the examples mentioned above.

DRAFTING

Write a paragraph in which you introduce the idea that you do/do not believe that *The Tempest* was Shakespeare's farewell.

In the body of your composition, write one paragraph for each of your reasons/arguments for/against *The Tempest* as Shakespeare's farewell. Use a topic sentence for each paragraph, stating your argument, and then fill out your paragraph with specific examples from the text.

Write a concluding paragraph in which you summarize your argument(s) and give your final comments on the issue.

PROMPT

When you finish the rough draft of your paper, ask a student who sits near you to read it. After reading your rough draft, he/she should tell you what he/she liked best about your work, which parts were difficult to understand, and ways in which your work could be improved. Reread your paper considering your critic's comments, and make the corrections you think are necessary.

REVIEW GAMES/ACTIVITIES - *Tempest*

1. Ask the class to make up a unit test for Tempest. The test should have 4 sections: matching, true/false, short answer, and essay. Students may use 1/2 period to make the test and then swap papers and use the other 1/2 class period to take a test a classmate has devised. (open book) You may want to use the unit test included in this packet or take questions from the students' unit tests to formulate your own test.

2. Take 1/2 period for students to make up true and false questions (including the answers). Collect the papers and divide the class into two teams. Draw a big tic-tac-toe board on the chalk board. Make one team X and one team O. Ask questions to each side, giving each student one turn. If the question is answered correctly, that students' team's letter (X or O) is placed in the box. If the answer is incorrect, no mark is placed in the box. The object is to get three marks in a row like tic-tac-toe. You may want to keep track of the number of games won for each team.

3. Take 1/2 period for students to make up questions (true/false and short answer). Collect the questions. Divide the class into two teams. You'll alternate asking questions to individual members of teams A & B (like in a spelling bee). The question keeps going from A to B until it is correctly answered, then a new question is asked. A correct answer does not allow the team to get another question. Correct answers are +2 points; incorrect answers are -1 point.

4. Have students pair up and quiz each other from their study guides and class notes.

5. Give students a *Tempest* crossword puzzle to complete.

6. Divide your class into two teams. Use the *Tempest* crossword words with their letters jumbled as a word list. Student 1 from Team A faces off against Student 1 from Team B. You write the first jumbled word on the board. The first student (1A or 1B) to unscramble the word wins the chance for his/her team to score points. If 1A wins the jumble, go to student 2A and give him/her a clue. He/she must give you the correct word which matches that clue. If he/she does, Team A scores a point, and you give student 3A a clue for which you expect another correct response. Continue giving Team A clues until some team member makes an incorrect response. An incorrect response sends the game back to the jumbled-word face off, this time with students 2A and 2B. Instead of repeating giving clues to the first few students of each team, continue with the student after the one who gave the last incorrect response on the team. For example, if Team B wins the jumbled-word face-off, and student 5B gave the last incorrect answer for Team B, you would start this round of clue questions with student 6B, and so on. The team with the most points wins!

UNIT TESTS

SHORT ANSWER UNIT TEST 1 - *The Tempest*

I. Matching/Identify

___ 1. Miranda   A. Rightful Duke of Milan

___ 2. Ceres   B. Spirit-servant to Prospero

___ 3. Antonio   C. Alonso's brother

___ 4. Prospero   D. Nobleman who helped Prospero by supplying boat

___ 5. Alonso   E. Prospero's deformed slave

___ 6. Ariel   F. King of Naples

___ 7. Sebastian   G. Prospero's daughter

___ 8. Ferdinand   H. A drunken butler

___ 9. Gonzalo   I. Goddess played by a spirit

___ 10. Caliban   J. Caliban's mother

___ 11. Stephano   K. Alonso's son

___ 12. Sycorax   L. Prospero's brother

II. Short Answer

1. How did Prospero and Miranda come to live on the island?

2. Who is Caliban?

Tempest Short Answer Unit Test 1 page 2

3. What do Anthony and Sebastian do while the others sleep?

4. Why does Caliban take up with Stephano and Trinculo?

5. What does Caliban want to do with Stephano and Trinculo while Prospero naps in the afternoon? Why?

6. Why does Prospero release the king's group?

7. What is ironic about Miranda's "brave new world" lines?

III. Essay

    What are three main themes in *The Tempest*? Write one paragraph for each of three main themes and explain each thoroughly.

The Tempest Short Answer Unit Test 1 Page 4

IV. Vocabulary

Listen to the vocabulary words and write them down. Go back later and fill in the correct definition for each word.

1.

2.

3.

4.

5.

6.

7.

8.

9.

10.

KEY: SHORT ANSWER UNIT TEST #1 - *The Tempest*

I. Matching/Identify]

__G__ 1. Miranda   A. Rightful Duke of Milan

__I__ 2. Ceres   B. Spirit-servant to Prospero

__L__ 3. Antonio   C. Alonso's brother

__A__ 4. Prospero   D. Nobleman who helped Prospero by supplying boat

__F__ 5. Alonso   E. Prospero's deformed slave

__B__ 6. Ariel   F. King of Naples

__C__ 7. Sebastian   G. Prospero's daughter

__K__ 8. Ferdinand   H. A drunken butler

__D__ 9. Gonzalo   I. Goddess played by a spirit

__E__ 10. Caliban   J. Caliban's mother

__H__ 11. Stephano   K. Alonso's son

__J__ 12. Sycorax   L. Prospero's brother

II. Short Answer

1. How did Prospero and Miranda come to live on the island?

   Prospero's brother Antonio and Alonso, King of Naples, conspired and overthrew Prospero. Prospero and his daughter Miranda were cast out. Gonzalo, the nobleman assigned to set them off, felt sorry for them and packed their boat with provisions. Some time later their boat was cast upon the shore of the island.

2. Who is Caliban?

> He is the son of the bad witch Sycorax. Through his magic, Prospero has made Caliban, a deformed, bestial human, his slave. Prospero taught Caliban and treated him kindly until Caliban tried to rape Miranda. Since then, Caliban has grown resentful of rough treatment and Prospero's taking over the island.

3. What do Anthony and Sebastian do while the others sleep?

> Anthony suggested that Sebastian should kill Alonso while he was sleeping. Sebastian said, "As thou got'st Milan,/I'll come by Naples. Draw thy sword."

4. Why does Caliban take up with Stephano and Trinculo?

> He meets them in the woods and mistakes the drunken Stephano for a god. Thinking Stephano will be able to defeat Prospero, and being disenchanted with Prospero, he decides to side with Stephano.

5. What does Caliban want to do with Stephano and Trinculo while Prospero naps in the afternoon? Why?

> He wants to kill Prospero while he sleeps so Stephano and Miranda can be King and Queen of the island with Caliban and Trinculo as lords.

6. Why does Prospero release the king's group?

> When giving the report about the party's well-being, Ariel mentioned "That if you now beheld them, your [Prospero's] affections/Would become tender." Prospero later decides "The rarer action is/In virtue than in vengeance."

7. What is ironic about Miranda's "brave new world" lines?

> The people she sees, whom she thinks represent a great humankind she has not known, are actually conspirators and would-be murderers.

III. Essay

> What are three main themes in *The Tempest*? Write one paragraph for each of three main themes and explain each thoroughly.

IV. Vocabulary

Choose ten of the following vocabulary words. Read them orally to your class so the students can write them down on part IV of their vocabulary tests.

ABHORRED	Abominable; loathsome
ABJURE	Give up; forswear
ALLAYING	Calming; relieving
ARDOR	Fiery intensity; strong enthusiasm
AUSPICIOUS	Favorable
AUSTERELY	Severely
BLASPHEMOUS	Irreverent
CONFEDERATES	Allies; comrades; accomplices
DILIGENT	Marked by perseverance
DISDAIN	Contempt; scorn
DOLOR	Grief; sorrow
EBB	Decline; flowing away
ENDOWED	Equipped; supplied
ENMITY	Deep hatred
EXPEDITIOUS	Done with speed and efficiency
INSOLENT	Insulting in manner; rude; impertinent
INVULNERABLE	Unable to be damaged; impenetrable
IRREPARABLE	Unable to be fixed
ODIOUS	Arousing strong dislike or displeasure
OMIT	Leave out
ORACLE	A wise person or a source of wisdom
PENITENT	Remorseful; sorry
PERDITION	Utter ruin; eternal damnation
PERFIDIOUS	Treacherous
PRATE	Chatter
PRECEPTS	Rules; principles
PROMONTORY	A high ridge of rock jutting into the water
SANCTIMONIOUS	Religious
SANS	Without
SCURVY	Contemptible
SUBTLE	Slight; difficult to detect
SUPPLANT	Displace and substitute
SURFEITED	Overfilled
TABOR	A small drum
USURP	Take over without legal authority
VEXATIONS	Annoyances; troubles
VEXED	Troubled; annoyed; bothered
VIGILANCE	Watchfulness
WANTON	Lewd; excessive

SHORT ANSWER UNIT TEST 2 - *The Tempest*

I. Matching/Identify

___ 1. Miranda   A. Spirit-servant to Prospero

___ 2. Ceres   B. Alonso's brother

___ 3. Antonio   C. Prospero's brother

___ 4. Prospero   D. Alonso's son

___ 5. Alonso   E. Prospero's daughter

___ 6. Ariel   F. Caliban's mother

___ 7. Sebastian   G. Prospero's deformed slave

___ 8. Ferdinand   H. Nobleman who helped Prospero by supplying boat

___ 9. Gonzalo   I. King of Naples

___ 10. Caliban   J. Goddess played by a spirit

___ 11. Stephano   K. A drunken butler

___ 12. Sycorax   L. Rightful Duke of Milan

II. Short Answer

1. Who is Ferdinand, and what happens when he meets Miranda? Why is that important to the theme(s) of the play?

2. What do Anthony and Sebastian do while the others sleep?

Tempest Short Answer Unit Test 2 page 2

3. Why does Caliban take up with Stephano and Trinculo?

4. What does Caliban want to do with Stephano and Trinculo while Prospero naps in the afternoon? Why?

5. What tricks do Prospero and Ariel play on Caliban, Stephano, and Trinculo?

6. Why does Prospero release the king's group?

7. What is Prospero's reaction when Alonso tries to apologize to Miranda for sending her and her father away?

8. What is ironic about Miranda's "brave new world" lines?

Tempest Short Answer Unit Test 2 page 3

III. Composition

    Explain the theme of illusion versus reality as it is exemplified in *The Tempest*.

IV. Vocabulary
    Listen to the vocabulary words and write them down. Go back later and fill in the correct definition for each word.

1.

2.

3.

4.

5.

6.

7.

8.

9.

10.

KEY: SHORT ANSWER UNIT TEST 2 *The Tempest*

I. Matching (Use this matching key also for the Advanced Short Answer Unit Test)

E	1. Miranda	A.	Spirit-servant to Prospero
J	2. Ceres	B.	Alonso's brother
C	3. Antonio	C.	Prospero's brother
L	4. Prospero	D.	Alonso's son
I	5. Alonso	E.	Prospero's daughter
A	6. Ariel	F.	Caliban's mother
B	7. Sebastian	G.	Prospero's deformed slave
D	8. Ferdinand	H.	Nobleman who helped Prospero by supplying boat
H	9. Gonzalo	I.	King of Naples
G	10. Caliban	J.	Goddess played by a spirit
K	11. Stephano	K.	A drunken butler
F	12. Sycorax	L.	Rightful Duke of Milan

II. Short Answer

1. Who is Ferdinand, and what happens when he meets Miranda? Why is that important to the theme(s) of the play?

    He is the son of the King of Naples. When Ferdinand and Miranda meet, they instantly fall in love. The uniting of Ferdinand and Miranda ends the discord between the two families. Shakespeare shows again the hope that the younger generation brings for the redemption of the older generation and the hope for a better future for mankind.

2. What do Anthony and Sebastian do while the others sleep?

    Anthony suggested that Sebastian should kill Alonso while he was sleeping. Sebastian said, "As thou got'st Milan,/I'll come by Naples. Draw thy sword."

3. Why does Caliban take up with Stephano and Trinculo?

    He meets them in the woods and mistakes the drunken Stephano for a god. Thinking Stephano will be able to defeat Prospero, and being disenchanted with Prospero, he decides to side with Stephano.

4. What does Caliban want to do with Stephano and Trinculo while Prospero naps in the afternoon? Why?

    He wants to kill Prospero while he sleeps so Stephano and Miranda can be King and Queen of the island with Caliban and Trinculo as lords.

5. What tricks do Prospero and Ariel play on Caliban, Stephano, and Trinculo?

    First Ariel leads them through briars and thorns and leaves them in a dirty pond. Then Prospero has Ariel put out "glistening" clothes for them (as bait). Finally, Prospero has spirits in the form of dogs chase the three away.

6. Why does Prospero release the king's group?

    When giving the report about the party's well-being, Ariel mentioned "That if you now beheld them, your [Prospero's] affections/Would become tender." Prospero later decides "The rarer action is/In virtue than in vengeance."

7. What is Prospero's reaction when Alonso tries to apologize to Miranda for sending her and her father away?

    Prospero says, "Let us not burden our remembrances with/A heaviness that's gone." In other words, he wants the past to be done and to start fresh.

8. What is ironic about Miranda's "brave new world" lines?

    The people she sees, whom she thinks represent a great humankind she has not known, are actually conspirators and would-be murderers.

III. Composition

    Discuss at two different kinds of humor Shakespeare uses in *The Tempest*. Use specific examples from the text to support your statements.

IV. Vocabulary

    Use the list from part IV of Short Answer Unit Test 1. Choose ten words and read them orally to your class so students can write them down.

ADVANCED SHORT ANSWER UNIT TEST - *The Tempest*

I. Matching

___ 1. Miranda   A. Spirit-servant to Prospero

___ 2. Ceres   B. Alonso's brother

___ 3. Antonio   C. Prospero's brother

___ 4. Prospero   D. Alonso's son

___ 5. Alonso   E. Prospero's daughter

___ 6. Ariel   F. Caliban's mother

___ 7. Sebastian   G. Prospero's deformed slave

___ 8. Ferdinand   H. Nobleman who helped Prospero by supplying boat

___ 9. Gonzalo   I. King of Naples

___ 10. Caliban   J. Goddess played by a spirit

___ 11. Stephano   K. A drunken butler

___ 12. Sycorax   L. Rightful Duke of Milan

II. Short Answer

1. What are the main conflicts in the play, and how are they resolved?

2. Explain how Shakespeare uses Ariel in the play and the effect of Ariel on the play.

The Tempest Advanced Short Answer Unit Test Page 2

3. Define "tragedy," "comedy," and "romance" in the theatrical/literary senses of the words and explain into what category or categories *The Tempest* falls.

4. Explain the idea of innocence versus experience as it relates to the play.

5. Compare and contrast Caliban and Ariel.

The Tempest Advanced Short Answer Unit Test Page 3

6. After the shipwreck, the passengers become separated into groups on the island. Compare and contrast the experiences of the groups: 1.) Alonso, Sebastian and Antonio 2.) Ferdinand 3.) Stephano and Trinculo.

7. What is Caliban's role in the play? What is the significance of his name? His physical characteristics?

8. Explain Caliban's relationship to Prospero in the play, both literally and symbolically/thematically.

The Tempest Advanced Short Answer Unit Test Page 4

III. Composition

    Which character would you choose as the central character of the play? Defend your choice using specific examples from the text and keeping in mind the themes of the play.

The Tempest Advanced Short Answer Unit Test Page 5

III. Vocabulary

Write down the vocabulary words you are given. Go back later and use all of those vocabulary words in a composition relating to *The Tempest*.

MULTIPLE CHOICE UNIT TEST 1 - *The Tempest*

I. Matching/Identify

___ 1. Miranda   A. Rightful Duke of Milan

___ 2. Ceres   B. Spirit-servant to Prospero

___ 3. Antonio   C. Alonso's brother

___ 4. Prospero   D. Nobleman who helped Prospero by supplying boat

___ 5. Alonso   E. Prospero's deformed slave

___ 6. Ariel   F. King of Naples

___ 7. Sebastian   G. Prospero's daughter

___ 8. Ferdinand   H. A drunken butler

___ 9. Gonzalo   I. Goddess played by a spirit

___ 10. Caliban   J. Caliban's mother

___ 11. Stephano   K. Alonso's son

___ 12. Sycorax   L. Prospero's brother

II. Multiple Choice

1. How did Prospero and Miranda come to live on the island?
    A. Prospero's brother Antonio and Alonso, the King of Naples, conspired and overthrew Prospero. Prospero and his daughter Miranda, were cast out. Gonzalo, the nobleman assigned to set them off, felt sorry for them and packed their boat with provisions. The boat was later cast upon the island.
    B. Prospero felt it was time to retire and leave the work of governing to his son. His daughter, Miranda, offered to come to the island with him and help him get settled.
    C. Miranda was being courted by a man she didn't want to marry. In order to protect her, her father took her to the island. At the same time, he had arranged for his soldiers to kill the suitor.
    D. Prospero had contracted a mysterious degenerative disease. The doctors didn't know how to cure it. Fearing that he was contagious, they banned him from his homeland, and sent him to the island to live. His daughter, Miranda, went along to nurse him.

The Tempest Multiple Choice Unit Test 1 Page 2

2. Which of the following statements does not describe Caliban?
    A. He is the son of the bad witch Sycorax.
    B. He is deformed and bestial-looking.
    C. He is highly intelligent, although he doesn't show it.
    D. He is Prospero's slave.

3. Who says the following lines, and who is being spoken about? "They are both in either's powers. But this is swift business/ I must uneasy make, lest too light winning/Make light the prize."
    A. Prospero is talking about Ferdinand and Miranda.
    B. The King of Naples is talking about winning the war against Antonio.
    C. Caliban is talking about Prospero and Ferdinand.
    D. Miranda is talking about Ferdinand and Alonso.

4. What do Anthony and Sebastian do while the others sleep?
    A. They steal Prospero's fortune.
    B. They attack Miranda.
    C. They conspire with Caliban.
    D. They plot to kill Alonso.

5. True or False: Caliban meets Stephano and Trinculo in the woods, and mistakes Stephano for a god. Thinking Stephano will be able to defeat Prospero, and being disenchanted with Prospero, he decides to side with Stephano.
    A. True
    B. False

6. What do Ferdinand and Miranda decide to do in Scene One?
    A. They decide to kill Alonso.
    B. They decide to get married.
    C. They decide to steal a boat and leave the island.
    D. They decide to force the others to have a peace talk.

7. What does Caliban want to do with Stephano and Trinculo while Prospero naps in the afternoon and why?
    A. He wants to kidnap them and hold them for ransom so he can get rich.
    B. He wants them to steal Prospero's money and a boat so they can get off the island.
    C. He wants them to collect all of the driftwood, including the remains of the ship, so they can build a huge signal fire.
    D. He wants to kill Prospero while he sleeps so Stephano and Miranda can be King and Queen of the island with Caliban and Trinculo as lords.

The Tempest Multiple Choice Unit Test 1 Page 3

8. What tricks do Prospero and Ariel play on Alonso's group?
    A. Prospero and Ariel make the members of the group think they all have animal heads.
    B. Prospero makes them thing they can hear each other's thoughts. Ariel makes them fall in love with each other.
    C. Prospero shows them a feast and then makes it disappear. Ariel reminds them of their sins, their injustices towards Prospero.
    D. Prospero creates a huge storm and makes them think they are all going to drown. Ariel makes them selfish and unwilling to help each other.

9. For what purpose did Prospero produce the spirits to play Iris, Ceres, and Juno?
    A. He wanted to scare the others into leaving him alone.
    B. He needed help to get rid of his tormentors.
    C. He wanted them to entertain at a celebration he had planned.
    D. He wanted them to protect Miranda from the evil men on the island.

10. What are Prospero and Ariel talking about in the following quotes: "That if you now beheld them, your affections/Would become tender." "The rarer action is/In virtue than in vengeance."
    A. Ariel thinks Prospero should let Miranda make her own decisions.
    B. Ariel thinks Prospero should release the king's group.

11. Who says "Let us not burden our remembrances with/A heaviness that's gone."?
    A. Ariel says it.
    B. Miranda says it.
    C. Alonso says it.
    D. Prospero says it.

12. What is ironic about Miranda's "brave new world" lines?
    A. She is not really brave at all.
    B. The people that she thinks represent a great humankind are really conspirators and would-be murderers.
    C. She doesn't know that her father said the same thing twenty years earlier.
    D. The explorers of the times are really on the verge of discovering "the New World"

The Tempest Multiple Choice Unit Test 1 Page 4

III. Composition

    Describe Caliban's relationship with Prospero and explain the importance of their relationship as it relates to the themes of the play.

The Tempest Multiple Choice Unit Test 1 Page 5

IV. Vocabulary - Match the correct definitions to the vocabulary words.

____ 1. EXPEDITIOUS   A. Remorseful; sorry

____ 2. PERFIDIOUS   B. Arousing strong dislike or displeasure

____ 3. PENITENT   C. Contempt; scorn

____ 4. ODIOUS   D. Irreverent

____ 5. DISDAIN   E. Religious

____ 6. PRECEPTS   F. Done with speed and efficiency

____ 7. SURFEITED   G. Take over without legal authority

____ 8. VEXATIONS   H. Annoyances; troubles

____ 9. AUSPICIOUS   I. Contemptible

____ 10. ALLAYING   J. Favorable

____ 11. ENDOWED   K. Severely

____ 12. BLASPHEMOUS   L. Leave out

____ 13. PRATE   M. Chatter

____ 14. DILIGENT   N. Equipped; supplied

____ 15. SCURVY   O. Marked by perseverance

____ 16. USURP   P. Rules; principles

____ 17. SANCTIMONIOUS   Q. Decline; flowing away

____ 18. EBB   R. Calming; relieving

____ 19. OMIT   S. Overfilled

____ 20. AUSTERELY   T. Treacherous

MULTIPLE CHOICE UNIT TEST 2 - *The Tempest*

I. Matching/Identify

___ 1. Miranda   A. Spirit-servant to Prospero

___ 2. Ceres   B. Alonso's brother

___ 3. Antonio   C. Prospero's brother

___ 4. Prospero   D. Alonso's son

___ 5. Alonso   E. Prospero's daughter

___ 6. Ariel   F. Caliban's mother

___ 7. Sebastian   G. Prospero's deformed slave

___ 8. Ferdinand   H. Nobleman who helped Prospero by supplying boat

___ 9. Gonzalo   I. King of Naples

___ 10. Caliban   J. Goddess played by a spirit

___ 11. Stephano   K. A drunken butler

___ 12. Sycorax   L. Rightful Duke of Milan

The Tempest Multiple Choice Unit Test 2 Page 2

II. Multiple Choice

1. How did Prospero and Miranda come to live on the island?
    A. Miranda was being courted by a man she didn't want to marry. In order to protect her, her father took her to the island. At the same time, he had arranged for his soldiers to kill the suitor.
    B. Prospero had contracted a mysterious degenerative disease. The doctors didn't know how to cure it. Fearing that he was contagious, they banned him from his homeland, and sent him to the island to live. His daughter, Miranda, went along to nurse him.
    C. Prospero's brother Antonio and Alonso, the King of Naples, conspired and overthrew Prospero. Prospero and his daughter Miranda, were cast out. Gonzalo, the nobleman assigned to set them off, felt sorry for them and packed their boat with provisions. The boat was later cast upon the island.
    D. Prospero felt it was time to retire and leave the work of governing to his son. His daughter, Miranda, offered to come to the island with him and help him get settled.

2. Which of the following statements does not describe Caliban?
    A. He is Prospero's slave.
    B. He is deformed and bestial-looking.
    C. He is the son of the bad witch Sycorax.
    D. He is highly intelligent, although he doesn't show it.

3. Who says the following lines, and who is being spoken about? "They are both in either's powers. But this is swift business/ I must uneasy make, lest too light winning/Make light the prize."
    A. Miranda is talking about Ferdinand and Alonso.
    B. Prospero is talking about Ferdinand and Miranda.
    C. The King of Naples is talking about winning the war against Antonio.
    D. Caliban is talking about Prospero and Ferdinand.

4. What do Anthony and Sebastian do while the others sleep?
    A. They plot to kill Alonso.
    B. They attack Miranda.
    C. They steal Prospero's fortune.
    D. They conspire with Caliban.

5. True or False: Caliban meets Stephano and Trinculo in the woods, and mistakes Stephano for a god. He hurries back to warn Prospero and to swear his allegiance to him.
    A. True
    B. False

The Tempest Multiple Choice Unit Test 2 Page 3

6. What do Ferdinand and Miranda decide to do in Scene One?
    A. They decide to force the others to have a peace talk.
    B. They decide to kill Alonso.
    C. They decide to get married.
    D. They decide to steal a boat and leave the island.

7. What does Caliban want to do with Stephano and Trinculo while Prospero naps in the afternoon and why?
    A. He wants to kill Prospero while he sleeps so Stephano and Miranda can be King and Queen of the island with Caliban and Trinculo as lords.
    B. He wants them to steal Prospero's money and a boat so they can get off the island.
    C. He wants them to collect all of the driftwood, including the remains of the ship, so they can build a huge signal fire.
    D. He wants to kidnap them and hold them for ransom so he can get rich.

8. What tricks do Prospero and Ariel play on Alonso's group?
    A. Prospero and Ariel make the members of the group think they all have animal heads.
    B. Prospero shows them a feast and then makes it disappear. Ariel reminds them of their sins, their injustices towards Prospero.
    C. Prospero creates a huge storm and makes them think they are all going to drown. Ariel makes them selfish and unwilling to help each other.
    D. Prospero makes them thing they can hear each other's thoughts. Ariel makes them fall in love with each other.

9. For what purpose did Prospero produce the spirits to play Iris, Ceres, and Juno?
    A. He wanted them to protect Miranda from the evil men on the island.
    B. He needed help to get rid of his tormentors.
    C. He wanted to scare the others into leaving him alone.
    D. He wanted them to entertain at a celebration he had planned.

10. What are Prospero and Ariel talking about in the following quotes: "That if you now beheld them, your affections/Would become tender." "The rarer action is/In virtue than in vengeance."
    A. Ariel thinks Prospero should release the king's group.
    B. Ariel thinks Prospero should let Miranda make her own decisions.

The Tempest Multiple Choice Unit Test 2 Page 4

11. Who says "Let us not burden our remembrances with/A heaviness that's gone."?
    A. Miranda says it.
    B. Ariel says it.
    C. Prospero says it.
    D. Alonso says it.

12. What is ironic about Miranda's "brave new world" lines?
    A. She is not really brave at all.
    B. She doesn't know that her father said the same thing twenty years earlier.
    C. The people that she thinks represent a great humankind are really conspirators and would-be murderers.
    D. The explorers of the times are really on the verge of discovering "the New World"

III. Composition
    Explain how *The Tempest* has the elements of comedy, tragedy and romance all in one play.

The Tempest Multiple Choice Unit Test 2 Page 6

IV. Vocabulary

____ 1. TABOR   A. Abominable; loathsome

____ 2. IRREPARABLE   B. Arousing strong dislike or displeasure

____ 3. ORACLE   C. Calming; relieving

____ 4. DISDAIN   D. Remorseful; sorry

____ 5. ARDOR   E. Grief; sorrow

____ 6. PERFIDIOUS   F. Favorable

____ 7. ABHORRED   G. Without

____ 8. ENMITY   H. Treacherous

____ 9. INSOLENT   I. Severely

____ 10. DOLOR   J. Unable to be fixed

____ 11. SURFEITED   K. Insulting in manner; rude; impertinent

____ 12. SCURVY   L. Done with speed and efficiency

____ 13. PENITENT   M. Contemptible

____ 14. EXPEDITIOUS   N. A small drum

____ 15. AUSTERELY   O. Overfilled

____ 16. AUSPICIOUS   P. Fiery intensity; strong enthusiasm

____ 17. ODIOUS   Q. Deep hatred

____ 18. ALLAYING   R. Contempt; scorn

____ 19. INVULNERABLE   S. A wise person or a source of wisdom

____ 20. SANS   T. Unable to be damaged; impenetrable

ANSWER SHEET - *The Tempest*
Multiple Choice Unit Tests

I. Matching
1. ___
2. ___
3. ___
4. ___
5. ___
6. ___
7. ___
8. ___
9. ___
10. ___
11. ___
12. ___

II. Multiple Choice
1. (A) (B) (C) (D)
2. (A) (B) (C) (D)
3. (A) (B) (C) (D)
4. (A) (B) (C) (D)
5. (A) (B) (C) (D)
6. (A) (B) (C) (D)
7. (A) (B) (C) (D)
8. (A) (B) (C) (D)
9. (A) (B) (C) (D)
10. (A) (B) (C) (D)
11. (A) (B) (C) (D)
12. (A) (B) (C) (D)

IV. Vocabulary
1. ___
2. ___
3. ___
4. ___
5. ___
6. ___
7. ___
8. ___
9. ___
10. ___
11. ___
12. ___
13. ___
14. ___
15. ___
16. ___
17. ___
18. ___
19. ___
20. ___

ANSWER SHEET KEY - *The Tempest*
Multiple Choice Unit Test 1

I. Matching
1. G
2. I
3. L
4. A
5. F
6. B
7. C
8. K
9. D
10. E
11. H
12. J

II. Multiple Choice
1. ( ) (B) (C) (D)
2. (A) (B) ( ) (D)
3. ( ) (B) (C) (D)
4. (A) (B) (C) ( )
5. ( ) (B) (C) (D)
6. (A) ( ) (C) (D)
7. (A) (B) (C) ( )
8. (A) (B) ( ) (D)
9. (A) (B) ( ) (D)
10. (A) ( ) (C) (D)
11. (A) (B) (C) ( )
12. (A) ( ) (C) (D)

IV. Vocabulary
1. F
2. T
3. A
4. B
5. C
6. P
7. S
8. H
9. J
10. R
11. N
12. D
13. M
14. O
15. I
16. G
17. E
18. Q
19. L
20. K

ANSWER SHEET KEY - *The Tempest*
Multiple Choice Unit Test 2

I. Matching
1.   E
2.   J
3.   C
4.   L
5.   I
6.   A
7.   B
8.   D
9.   H
10.   G
11.   K
12.   F

II. Multiple Choice
1. (A) (B) ( ) (D)
2. (A) (B) (C) ( )
3. (A) ( ) (C) (D)
4. ( ) (B) (C) (D)
5. (A) ( ) (C) (D)
6. (A) (B) ( ) (D)
7. ( ) (B) (C) (D)
8. (A) ( ) (C) (D)
9. (A) (B) (C) ( )
10. ( ) (B) (C) (D)
11. (A) (B) ( ) (D)
12. (A) (B) ( ) (D)

IV. Vocabulary
1.   N
2.   J
3.   S
4.   R
5.   P
6.   H
7.   A
8.   Q
9.   K
10.   E
11.   O
12.   M
13.   D
14.   L
15.   I
16.   P
17.   B
18.   C
19.   T
20.   G

UNIT RESOURCE MATERIALS

BULLETIN BOARD IDEAS - *The Tempest*

1. Save one corner of the board for the best of students' *The Tempest* writing assignments.

2. Take one of the word search puzzles from the extra activities packet and with a marker copy it over in a large size on the bulletin board. Write the clue words to find to one side. Invite students prior to and after class to find the words and circle them on the bulletin board.

3. Write several of the most significant quotations from the book onto the board on brightly colored paper.

4. Make a bulletin board listing the vocabulary words for this unit. As you complete sections of the novel and discuss the vocabulary for each section, write the definitions on the bulletin board. (If your board is one students face frequently, it will help them learn the words.)

5. Make a bulletin board about courtship and marriage. Post articles and pictures from our own culture, Shakespeare's times, or about various cultures from around the world.

6. Post articles of criticism about the play.

7. Do a bulletin board about Shakespeare. Post a brief summary of his life next to his picture. All around the bulletin board, post "playbills" for each of his major works with a little summary of the plot of each play written inside.

8. As an alternate introductory activity, prepare a bulletin board with the title SHAKESPEARE on background paper with his picture in the middle of the board. Ask each student to write one fact, the title of a play, a quote, or anything he/she knows relating to Shakespeare.

9. Title the board: THE TEMPEST: SHAKESPEARE'S FAREWELL? Copy the Epilogue onto the bulletin board.

10. Find a book of visual illusions. Cut it apart and post the various illusions on the board.

EXTRA ACTIVITIES - *The Tempest*

One of the difficulties in teaching a novel is that all students don't read at the same speed. One student who likes to read may take the book home and finish it in a day or two. Sometimes a few students finish the in-class assignments early. The problem, then, is finding suitable extra activities for students.

One thing that helps is to keep a little library in the classroom. For this unit on *The Tempest*, you might check out from the school library other plays by Shakespeare. A biography or articles about the author would be interesting for some students. You can include other books and articles about courtship and marriage, dreams and dreaming, fairies, history of the period, careers in the theater, gods and goddesses, natives, articles about Shakespearian/Elizabethan theater, or articles of criticism about *The Tempest*.

Other things you may keep on hand are puzzles. We have made some relating directly to *The Tempest* for you. Feel free to duplicate them for your students.

Some students may like to draw. You might devise a contest or allow some extra-credit grade for students who draw characters or scenes from *The Tempest*. Note, too, that if the students do not want to keep their drawings you may pick up some extra bulletin board materials this way. If you have a contest and you supply the prize (a CD or something like that perhaps), you could, possibly, make the drawing itself a non-refundable entry fee.

The pages which follow contain games, puzzles and worksheets. The keys, when appropriate, immediately follow the puzzle or worksheet. There are two main groups of activities: one group for the unit; that is, generally relating to the *Tempest* text, and another group of activities related strictly to the *Tempest* vocabulary.

Directions for these games, puzzles and worksheets are self-explanatory. The object here is to provide you with extra materials you may use in any way you choose.

MORE ACTIVITIES - *The Tempest*

1. Have students design a playbill for *The Tempest*.

2. Have students design a bulletin board (ready to be put up) for *The Tempest*.

3. Use some of the related topics (noted earlier for an in-class library) as topics for research, reports or written papers, or as topics for guest speakers.

4. Invite a marriage counselor in to talk to students about courtship and marriage in our society today.

5. Research courtship in the 1600s and/or the history of courtship through the ages.

6. Instead of making a whole production, assign a character to each student. Have students design their own costumes, memorize a short passage from the play, and recite the passage (in costume) in front of the class.

7. Compare and contrast *The Tempest* with a modern romantic comedy/drama about love.

8. After analyzing Shakespeare's poetry, have students experiment imitating his style by rewriting the end of the play.

9. Have students research careers in the theater, acting, and movies as well as careers related to courtship and marriage (preacher, dating service, tuxedo rental business, catering, floral shop, etc.).

10. Find a film version of *The Tempest*, show it, and compare/contrast it with the written play.

11. Read *Brave New World*. Compare and contrast the themes in it with those in *The Tempest*.

WORD SEARCH - *The Tempest*

All words in this list are associated with *The Tempest*. The words are placed backwards, forward, diagonally, up and down. The included words are listed below the word searches.

```
Y P W R P F V B R R X N B G Q P X J X
J N K A G K O K P J Q H T L S C K F D D
F W P S O G Q N X B N V E S B S J Z C X
F E R D I N A N D R Q I G I F T H R S S
T J A S Q M A E H H R G A M W G X E Z N
Z N D S L C I H L A S G G W O N L S H F
N M T G T R O S P Z S C H R S P B E B D
A D N A R I M T S E P M E T A T R X L Z
Z V N A N G M E B N T P B N C A A L L Y
T H M O R W R A X L S S V A E S I O C N
L N T X H E S Y C O R A X P N K L O B V
K N P J C T F N R J Z Z S A B A S A W C
A M Q V I G D P X C S E B K Z N K W V Q
P H F A Z F L H S Y K I G N O Z B D Z E
F N N P F Y S H J A L C O L J T F D D W
F X J L Q Z B J H A N G A W Z G Y Z V Z
D C S G V H L S C N C S B Q W D X K S N
D D T S M Z J G X C D H W V C M G K P N
```

ACT	FEAST	NAPLES	SLAVE
ALONSO	FERDINAND	POND	STEPHANO
ANTONIO	GIFT	PROSPERO	SYCORAX
ARIEL	GONZALO	RAPE	TEMPEST
BOATSWAIN	KILL	SCENE	
CALIBAN	MARRIED	SEBASTIAN	
CERES	MIRANDA	SHAKESPEARE	

KEY: WORD SEARCH - *The Tempest*

All words in this list are associated with *The Tempest*. The words are placed backwards, forward, diagonally, up and down. The included words are listed below the word searches.

```
                  R P
              A     O                            L
      F   P   O   N     N   E
      F E R D I N A N D       I   G I F T         S
          A       A E         R   A               E
          S       I H   A S       W   O   L
              T R O   P   S C     R S P       E
      A D N A R I M T S E P M E T A T R       L
              A N     E B   T P   N C A A L
              M O     R A   S S   A E S I O
                T     E S Y C O R A X P N K L O B
          N       C T     R         S A   A S A
      A           I       P         E B   Z N       V
                  A                 K I   N O             E
              N                   A L   O L
                                  H A G A
                                  S C
```

ACT	FEAST	NAPLES	SLAVE
ALONSO	FERDINAND	POND	STEPHANO
ANTONIO	GIFT	PROSPERO	SYCORAX
ARIEL	GONZALO	RAPE	TEMPEST
BOATSWAIN	KILL	SCENE	
CALIBAN	MARRIED	SEBASTIAN	
CERES	MIRANDA	SHAKESPEARE	

CROSSWORD - *The Tempest*

CROSSWORD CLUES *Tempest*

ACROSS
4. Ferdinand and Miranda decided to get ___
5. Alonso's brother
8. Prospero's brother
10. King of Naples
13. Spirit-servant to Prospero
16. Nobleman who helped Prospero by supplying a boat
17. Alonso's son
18. Goddess played by a spirit
20. Rightful Duke of Milan
21. Caliban's mother
22. Name of the play; The ___
23. Play division

DOWN
1. Prospero shows Alonso's group a ___ then makes it disappear
2. Miranda is Prospero's ___ to Ferdinand
3. A drunken butler
4. Prospero's daughter
6. He's rude to his passengers
7. Anthony suggested Sebastian should ___ Alonso while he slept
9. Alonso is King of ___
11. Author
12. Ariel leaves Cal., Steph, & Trin. there
14. Caliban tried to ___ Miranda
15. Act division
18. Prospero's deformed slave
19. Caliban to Prospero

CROSSWORD ANSWER KEY - *The Tempest*

Across answers visible in the grid:
- MARRIED
- SEBASTIAN
- ANTONIO
- ALONSO
- ARIEL
- FERDINAND
- GONZALO
- CERES
- PROSPERO
- SYCORAX
- TEMPEST
- ACT

Down answers visible in the grid:
- FEAST
- SEPHAN (STEPHANO)
- GIFT
- KOATLAWAID
- SHAKESPEARE
- FESTIVAL
- MIRANDAN
- RAPPL
- SC
- CALIBAN
- SLAVE
- FERNLE
- PLONKESD

110

MATCHING QUIZ/WORKSHEET 1 - *The Tempest*

____ 1. MARRIED   A. Alonso is King of ___

____ 2. FERDINAND   B. Play division

____ 3. KILL   C. Caliban's mother

____ 4. SYCORAX   D. Author

____ 5. TEMPEST   E. Anthony suggested Sebastian should ___ Alonso while he slept

____ 6. GONZALO   F. A drunken butler

____ 7. CERES   G. Prospero's deformed slave

____ 8. ARIEL   H. Prospero shows Alonso's group a ___ then makes it disappear

____ 9. STEPHANO   I. Prospero's daughter

____ 10. GIFT   J. Spirit-servant to Prospero

____ 11. SLAVE   K. Caliban tried to ___ Miranda

____ 12. ALONSO   L. Act division

____ 13. NAPLES   M. Name of the play; The ___

____ 14. RAPE   N. Caliban to Prospero

____ 15. SHAKESPEARE   O. Miranda is Prospero's ___ to Ferdinand

____ 16. SCENE   P. King of Naples

____ 17. CALIBAN   Q. Alonso's son

____ 18. FEAST   R. Goddess played by a spirit

____ 19. ACT   S. Ferdinand and Miranda decided to get ___

____ 20. MIRANDA   T. Nobleman who helped Prospero by supplying a boat

KEY: MATCHING QUIZ/WORKSHEET 1 - *The Tempest*

_S_ 1. MARRIED		A. Alonso is King of ___
_Q_ 2. FERDINAND		B. Play division
_E_ 3. KILL		C. Caliban's mother
_C_ 4. SYCORAX		D. Author
_M_ 5. TEMPEST		E. Anthony suggested Sebastian should ___ Alonso while he slept
_T_ 6. GONZALO		F. A drunken butler
_R_ 7. CERES		G. Prospero's deformed slave
_J_ 8. ARIEL		H. Prospero shows Alonso's group a ___ then makes it disappear
_F_ 9. STEPHANO		I. Prospero's daughter
_O_ 10. GIFT		J. Spirit-servant to Prospero
_N_ 11. SLAVE		K. Caliban tried to ___ Miranda
_P_ 12. ALONSO		L. Act division
_A_ 13. NAPLES		M. Name of the play; The ___
_K_ 14. RAPE		N. Caliban to Prospero
_D_ 15. SHAKESPEARE		O. Miranda is Prospero's ___ to Ferdinand
_L_ 16. SCENE		P. King of Naples
_G_ 17. CALIBAN		Q. Alonso's son
_H_ 18. FEAST		R. Goddess played by a spirit
_B_ 19. ACT		S. Ferdinand and Miranda decided to get ___
_I_ 20. MIRANDA		T. Nobleman who helped Prospero by supplying a boat

MATCHING QUIZ/WORKSHEET 2 - *The Tempest*

____ 1. SCENE   A. Prospero's deformed slave

____ 2. CALIBAN   B. King of Naples

____ 3. ARIEL   C. Nobleman who helped Prospero by supplying a boat

____ 4. MARRIED   D. Act division

____ 5. SEBASTIAN   E. Spirit-servant to Prospero

____ 6. GIFT   F. Ferdinand and Miranda decided to get ___

____ 7. MIRANDA   G. Miranda is Prospero's ___ to Ferdinand

____ 8. RAPE   H. He's rude to his passengers

____ 9. ANTONIO   I. Prospero's daughter

____ 10. STEPHANO   J. Caliban tried to ___ Miranda

____ 11. GONZALO   K. A drunken butler

____ 12. SYCORAX   L. Goddess played by a spirit

____ 13. PROSPERO   M. Alonso's brother

____ 14. TEMPEST   N. Rightful Duke of Milan

____ 15. ACT   O. Prospero's brother

____ 16. POND   P. Caliban to Prospero

____ 17. SLAVE   Q. Ariel leaves Cal., Steph, & Trin. there

____ 18. ALONSO   R. Play division

____ 19. CERES   S. Name of the play; The ___

____ 20. BOATSWAIN   T. Caliban's mother

KEY: MATCHING QUIZ/WORKSHEET 2 - *The Tempest*

__D_ 1. SCENE   A. Prospero's deformed slave

__A_ 2. CALIBAN   B. King of Naples

__E_ 3. ARIEL   C. Nobleman who helped Prospero by supplying a boat

__F_ 4. MARRIED   D. Act division

__M_ 5. SEBASTIAN   E. Spirit-servant to Prospero

__G_ 6. GIFT   F. Ferdinand and Miranda decided to get ___

__I_ 7. MIRANDA   G. Miranda is Prospero's ___ to Ferdinand

__J_ 8. RAPE   H. He's rude to his passengers

__O_ 9. ANTONIO   I. Prospero's daughter

__K_ 10. STEPHANO   J. Caliban tried to ___ Miranda

__C_ 11. GONZALO   K. A drunken butler

__T_ 12. SYCORAX   L. Goddess played by a spirit

__N_ 13. PROSPERO   M. Alonso's brother

__S_ 14. TEMPEST   N. Rightful Duke of Milan

__R_ 15. ACT   O. Prospero's brother

__Q_ 16. POND   P. Caliban to Prospero

__P_ 17. SLAVE   Q. Ariel leaves Cal., Steph, & Trin. there

__B_ 18. ALONSO   R. Play division

__L_ 19. CERES   S. Name of the play; The ___

__H_ 20. BOATSWAIN   T. Caliban's mother

JUGGLE LETTER REVIEW GAME CLUE SHEET - *The Tempest*

SCRAMBLED	WORD	CLUE
NARIMA	MIRANDA	Prospero's daughter
SCREE	CERES	Goddess played by a spirit
TOONINA	ANTONIO	Prospero's brother
SOOPREPR	PROSPERO	Rightful Duke of Milan
SOONAL	ALONSO	King of Naples
LEARI	ARIEL	Spirit-servant to Prospero
TESANIABS	SEBASTIAN	Alonso's brother
DANREFNID	FERDINAND	Alonso's son
LOGONZA	GONZALO	Nobleman who helped Prospero by supplying a boat
NALACIB	CALIBAN	Prospero's deformed slave
THONPEAS	STEPHANO	A drunken butler
XROCSYA	SYCORAX	Caliban's mother
WAITSABINO	BOATSWAIN	He's rude to his passengers
VALES	SLAVE	Caliban to Prospero
PARE	RAPE	Caliban tried to ___ Miranda
SLAPEN	NAPLES	Alonso is King of ___
LILK	KILL	Anthony suggested Sebastian should ___ Alonso while he slept
RAMDEIR	MARRIED	Ferdinand and Miranda decided to get ___
STEAF	FEAST	Prospero shows Alonso's group a ___ then makes it disappear
FITG	GIFT	Miranda is Prospero's ___ to Ferdinand
DOPN	POND	Ariel leaves Cal., Steph, & Trin. there
ERAEPSKEHAS	SHAKESPEARE	Author
TAC	ACT	Play division
NEECS	SCENE	Act division
PETMSET	TEMPEST	Name of the play; The ___

VOCABULARY RESOURCE MATERIALS

VOCABULARY WORD SEARCH - *The Tempest*

All words in this list are associated with *The Tempest* with an emphasis on the vocabulary words chosen for study in the text. The words are placed backwards, forward, diagonally, up and down. The included words are listed below.

```
N M E O S F C B R J Y P R I R J I Y T Y S P Y T
D B Y L M U T R J C R L K K R D V N G A T A H F
V E X A T I O N S U O I D I F R E P S B B E N E
T E T Z B B T I S U K N P I U D E W B O C O L S
S A X I W J U U C B O R F C S N I P O N L B R P
A Z R E E G U S R I A M S E I D S L A D A E P V
D L F D D F U R A T P X E T D U A L I R N C N L
D V L C O P R E E N L S E H O E I I E G A E P T
P O N A P R A U N H C N U I P G R N N S E B Q H
W P L L Y E A B S M T T T A I S L A U O W N L K
M G A O N I R C H P I I I V P U A O T S T T T E
F N W K R G N D L O D T X M V R I L Y E T N Y J
T Y S J X M P G I E R K Y N O D O S B Q S L A D
S P N T R B X H P T K R I L O N T M X X E J B W
Z R W F B S K X D V I T E Z C P I C O R W G L G
M X W Y R Z E S Z N Y O M D E Y W O E N J D X H
H H R C N F P P W R W Q N C J T G T U X T N F H
N W W J T M G W J G P Y E X F T S L D S M O X L
F F K Q Z F B V N R R R Q L J U Y M H J M D R F
Z P C X H W D J C G P N F J A D Q B R X J L N Y
```

ABHORRED	DOLOR	ORACLE	SUBTLE
ABJURE	EBB	PENITENT	SUPPLANT
ALLAYING	ENDOWED	PERDITION	SURFEITED
ARDOR	ENMITY	PERFIDIOUS	TABOR
AUSPICIOUS	EXPEDITIOUS	PRATE	USURP
AUSTERELY	INSOLENT	PRECEPTS	VEXATIONS
BLASPHEMOUS	INVULNERABLE	PROMONTORY	VEXED
CONFEDERATES	IRREPARABLE	SANCTIMONIOUS	VIGILANCE
DILIGENT	ODIOUS	SANS	WANTON
DISDAIN	OMIT	SCURVY	

KEY: VOCABULARY WORD SEARCH - *The Tempest*

All words in this list are associated with *The Tempest* with an emphasis on the vocabulary words chosen for study in the text. The words are placed backwards, forward, diagonally, up and down. The included words are listed below.

```
            E O S               P   I       I Y T     S
        D   L M U         C R         R D V N   A   A
        V E X A T I O N S U O I D I F R E P S B B E N E
          E T   B B T I S U   N P I U D E W   O C O L S
          A X   I   J U U C   O R F C S N I P O N L B R
        A   R E E   U S   I A M S E I D S L A D A E
            L   D D F U R A T P   E T D U A L I R N     N
        D   L   O P R E E N   S E H O E I I E G A E     T
            O   A P R A U N   C N U I P G R N N S E B
                L L Y E A B S M T T A I S L A U O   N L
                A O   I R C H   I I I V P U A O T   T   T E
              N     R   N D L O D T   M V R I L   E   N Y
            T           G I E R   Y N O D O S B   S L A
                          P T   R I   O N T M     E       W
                            X   I E       P I   O R
                          E         O   D E     O E N
                                      N C       T U   T
                                      E         S   S O
                                    R           U         R
                                  P           A           Y
```

ABHORRED   DOLOR   ORACLE   SUBTLE
ABJURE   EBB   PENITENT   SUPPLANT
ALLAYING   ENDOWED   PERDITION   SURFEITED
ARDOR   ENMITY   PERFIDIOUS   TABOR
AUSPICIOUS   EXPEDITIOUS   PRATE   USURP
AUSTERELY   INSOLENT   PRECEPTS   VEXATIONS
BLASPHEMOUS   INVULNERABLE   PROMONTORY   VEXED
CONFEDERATES   IRREPARABLE   SANCTIMONIOUS   VIGILANCE
DILIGENT   ODIOUS   SANS   WANTON
DISDAIN   OMIT   SCURVY

VOCABULARY CROSSWORD - *The Tempest*

VOCABULARY CROSSWORD CLUES - *The Tempest*

ACROSS
2. Irreverent
7. Miranda is Prospero's ___ to Ferdinand
9. Fiery intensity; strong enthusiasm
12. Spirit-servant to Prospero
13. Contemptible
15. Severely
18. Displace and substitute
19. Abominable; loathsome
22. One who lies
23. Acquire
24. Present plural of to be
25. Belonging to us
26. Goddess played by a spirit
27. Belonging to me
28. Grief; sorrow
29. Anthony suggested Sebastian should ___ Alonso while he slept
30. Troubled; annoyed; bothered
33. Every one
34. Insulting in manner; rude; impertinent
39. Coordinating conjunction
40. Take over without legal authority
41. Caliban tried to ___ Miranda
42. Opposite of under
43. Lewd; excessive
44. Rules; principles

DOWN
1. Prospero's 's deformed slave
3. Ariel leaves Cal., Steph, & Trin. there
4. Deep hatred
5. Arousing strong dislike or displeasure
6. Without
8. Unable to be damaged; impenetrable
9. Calming; relieving
10. Leave out
11. Favorable
12. Play division
14. Equipped; supplied
16. Religious
17. Decline; flowing away
19. Give up; forswear
20. A wise person or a source of wisdom
21. Done with speed and efficiency
27. Prospero's daughter
28. Marked by perseverance
31. Contempt; scorn
32. King of Naples
35. Slight; difficult to detect
36. A small drum
37. Alonso is King of ___
38. Chatter

VOCABULARY CROSSWORD ANSWER KEY - *The Tempest*

BLASPHEMOUS
GIFT
ARDOR
ARIEL
SCURVY
AUSTERELY
SUPPLANT
ABHORRED
LIAR
GET
ARE
OUR
CERES
MY
DOLOR
KILL
VEXED
ALL
INSOLENT
AND
USURP
RAPE
OVER
WANTON
PRECEPTS
CALIBAN
POND
ENMITY
ODIOUS
SANS
ACT
ALLAYING
SANCTIMONIOUS
AUSPICIOUS
INVULNERABLE
ENDOWED
EBB
ABJURE
ORACLE
EXPEDITIOUS
MIRANDA
DILIGENT
ALONSO
SUBTLE
TABOR
PRATE
NAPLES
DISDAIN

VOCABULARY WORKSHEET 1 - *The Tempest*

____ 1. Contempt; scorn
    A. Promontory   B. Disdain   C. Vexed   D. Enmity

____ 2. Chatter
    A. Prate   B. Endowed   C. Scurvy   D. Ebb

____ 3. Severely
    A. Abhorred   B. Scurvy   C. Austerely   D. Ebb

____ 4. Grief; sorrow
    A. Dolor   B. Usurp   C. Oracle   D. Vexed

____ 5. Marked by perseverance
    A. Diligent   B. Ardor   C. Ebb   D. Scurvy

____ 6. Annoyances; troubles
    A. Confederates   B. Vexations   C. Endowed   D. Sans

____ 7. Unable to be damaged; impenetrable
    A. Surfeited   B. Invulnerable   C. Abjure   D. Tabor

____ 8. Overfilled
    A. Sanctimonious   B. Ebb   C. Surfeited   D. Tabor

____ 9. Done with speed and efficiency
    A. Dolor   B. Expeditious   C. Invulnerable   D. Ebb

____ 10. Deep hatred
    A. Surfeited   B. Ardor   C. Enmity   D. Usurp

____ 11. Slight; difficult to detect
    A. Subtle   B. Sanctimonious   C. Wanton   D. Allaying

____ 12. Equipped; supplied
    A. Endowed   B. Vexed   C. Dolor   D. Sans

____ 13. Take over without legal authority
    A. Allaying   B. Usurp   C. Abjure   D. Supplant

____ 14. Remorseful; sorry
    A. Penitent   B. Precepts   C. Promontory   D. Vigilance

____ 15. Utter ruin; eternal damnation
    A. Perdition   B. Vigilance   C. Vexed   D. Surfeited

____ 16. Allies; comrades; accomplices
    A. Confederates   B. Odious   C. Austerely   D. Expeditious

____ 17. Leave out
    A. Confederates   B. Perfidious   C. Vexed   D. Omit

____ 18. Abominable; loathsome
    A. Supplant   B. Allaying   C. Vexed   D. Abhorred

____ 19. Fiery intensity; strong enthusiasm
    A. Ardor   B. Austerely   C. Irreparable   D. Promontory

____ 20. Irreverent
    A. Scurvy   B. Vexed   C. Blasphemous   D. Ardor

KEY: VOCABULARY WORKSHEET 1 - *The Tempest*

__B__ 1. Contempt; scorn
    A. Promontory   B. Disdain   C. Vexed   D. Enmity

__A__ 2. Chatter
    A. Prate   B. Endowed   C. Scurvy   D. Ebb

__C__ 3. Severely
    A. Abhorred   B. Scurvy   C. Austerely   D. Ebb

__A__ 4. Grief; sorrow
    A. Dolor   B. Usurp   C. Oracle   D. Vexed

__A__ 5. Marked by perseverance
    A. Diligent   B. Ardor   C. Ebb   D. Scurvy

__B__ 6. Annoyances; troubles
    A. Confederates   B. Vexations   C. Endowed   D. Sans

__B__ 7. Unable to be damaged; impenetrable
    A. Surfeited   B. Invulnerable   C. Abjure   D. Tabor

__C__ 8. Overfilled
    A. Sanctimonious   B. Ebb   C. Surfeited   D. Tabor

__B__ 9. Done with speed and efficiency
    A. Dolor   B. Expeditious   C. Invulnerable   D. Ebb

__C__ 10. Deep hatred
    A. Surfeited   B. Ardor   C. Enmity   D. Usurp

__A__ 11. Slight; difficult to detect
    A. Subtle   B. Sanctimonious   C. Wanton   D. Allaying

__A__ 12. Equipped; supplied
    A. Endowed   B. Vexed   C. Dolor   D. Sans

__B__ 13. Take over without legal authority
    A. Allaying   B. Usurp   C. Abjure   D. Supplant

__A__ 14. Remorseful; sorry
    A. Penitent   B. Precepts   C. Promontory   D. Vigilance

__A__ 15. Utter ruin; eternal damnation
    A. Perdition   B. Vigilance   C. Vexed   D. Surfeited

__A__ 16. Allies; comrades; accomplices
    A. Confederates   B. Odious   C. Austerely   D. Expeditious

__D__ 17. Leave out
    A. Confederates   B. Perfidious   C. Vexed   D. Omit

__D__ 18. Abominable; loathsome
    A. Supplant   B. Allaying   C. Vexed   D. Abhorred

__A__ 19. Fiery intensity; strong enthusiasm
    A. Ardor   B. Austerely   C. Irreparable   D. Promontory

__C__ 20. Irreverent
    A. Scurvy   B. Vexed   C. Blasphemous   D. Ardor

VOCABULARY WORKSHEET 2 - *The Tempest*

____ 1. ABHORRED   A. Marked by perseverance

____ 2. PERFIDIOUS   B. Displace and substitute

____ 3. PRATE   C. Watchfulness

____ 4. SANS   D. A wise person or a source of wisdom

____ 5. VEXED   E. Done with speed and efficiency

____ 6. VIGILANCE   F. Decline; flowing away

____ 7. EXPEDITIOUS   G. Grief; sorrow

____ 8. DILIGENT   H. Favorable

____ 9. ODIOUS   I. Unable to be fixed

____ 10. EBB   J. Arousing strong dislike or displeasure

____ 11. SUPPLANT   K. Without

____ 12. ENMITY   L. Troubled; annoyed; bothered

____ 13. SURFEITED   M. Contemptible

____ 14. AUSTERELY   N. Overfilled

____ 15. ORACLE   O. Treacherous

____ 16. IRREPARABLE   P. Deep hatred

____ 17. SCURVY   Q. Abominable; loathsome

____ 18. AUSPICIOUS   R. Utter ruin; eternal damnation

____ 19. DOLOR   S. Severely

____ 20. PERDITION   T. Chatter

KEY: VOCABULARY WORKSHEET 2 - *The Tempest*

_Q_ 1. ABHORRED		A. Marked by perseverance
_O_ 2. PERFIDIOUS		B. Displace and substitute
_T_ 3. PRATE		C. Watchfulness
_K_ 4. SANS		D. A wise person or a source of wisdom
_L_ 5. VEXED		E. Done with speed and efficiency
_C_ 6. VIGILANCE		F. Decline; flowing away
_E_ 7. EXPEDITIOUS		G. Grief; sorrow
_A_ 8. DILIGENT		H. Favorable
_J_ 9. ODIOUS		I. Unable to be fixed
_F_ 10. EBB		J. Arousing strong dislike or displeasure
_B_ 11. SUPPLANT		K. Without
_P_ 12. ENMITY		L. Troubled; annoyed; bothered
_N_ 13. SURFEITED		M. Contemptible
_S_ 14. AUSTERELY		N. Overfilled
_D_ 15. ORACLE		O. Treacherous
_I_ 16. IRREPARABLE		P. Deep hatred
_M_ 17. SCURVY		Q. Abominable; loathsome
_H_ 18. AUSPICIOUS		R. Utter ruin; eternal damnation
_G_ 19. DOLOR		S. Severely
_R_ 20. PERDITION		T. Chatter

VOCABULARY JUGGLE LETTER REVIEW GAME CLUES - *The Tempest*

SCRAMBLED	WORD	CLUE
REHABROD	ABHORRED	Abominable; loathsome
JAREBU	ABJURE	Give up; forswear
GALYLINA	ALLAYING	Calming; relieving
RROAD	ARDOR	Fiery intensity; strong enthusiasm
ISIUPAUOSC	AUSPICIOUS	Favorable
REELUTASY	AUSTERELY	Severely
SHOUPMALBES	BLASPHEMOUS	Irreverent
ODEENTRAFSEC	CONFEDERATES	Allies; comrades; accomplices
TIDELGIN	DILIGENT	Marked by perseverance
NADISID	DISDAIN	Contempt; scorn
ODORL	DOLOR	Grief; sorrow
BEB	EBB	Decline; flowing away
DWONEED	ENDOWED	Equipped; supplied
YENTIM	ENMITY	Deep hatred
DEESUOPIXIT	EXPEDITIOUS	Done with speed and efficiency
ITLONSEN	INSOLENT	Insulting in manner; rude; impertinent
ERVBNILUEAL	INVULNERABLE	Unable to be damaged; impenetrable
RAEPERBILAR	IRREPARABLE	Unable to be fixed
UDOOSI	ODIOUS	Arousing strong dislike or displeasure
MOIT	OMIT	Leave out
CAROLE	ORACLE	A wise person or a source of wisdom
INTEEPTN	PENITENT	Remorseful; sorry
EIDNITROP	PERDITION	Utter ruin; eternal damnation
FEOSIUDRIP	PERFIDIOUS	Treacherous
TAREP	PRATE	Chatter
CSTERPEP	PRECEPTS	Rules; principles
YOMTONRROP	PROMONTORY	A high ridge of rock jutting into the water
UNNICMOOTSAI	SANCTIMONIOUS	Religious
NSAS	SANS	Without
YCRUSV	SCURVY	Contemptible
BULETS	SUBTLE	Slight; difficult to detect
PLUSTANP	SUPPLANT	Displace and substitute
DREETUSIF	SURFEITED	Overfilled
BAROT	TABOR	A small drum
PURSU	USURP	Take over without legal authority
XENOIVATS	VEXATIONS	Annoyances; troubles
VXEED	VEXED	Troubled; annoyed; bothered
LINAGECIV	VIGILANCE	Watchfulness
NOTNAW	WANTON	Lewd; excessive

www.ingramcontent.com/pod-product-compliance
Lightning Source LLC
Chambersburg PA
CBHW051416070526
44584CB00023B/3456